Living I

Grief

&

Hope

Leah Bucko

Written in memory of my precious son,
Reuben Josiah,
and my darling mum,
Christina Jeffery.

Contents

Section 5: Leading

Foreword

This is a brave, inspiring, raw, and emotional book about the tragic loss of a beloved baby, but one which tracks the emergence of a hard-won wisdom for life, without minimising the pain the author went through with her family.

We learn that we cannot have a life free from pain and suffering. That it's ok to lament and question God.

The author is realistic about the rollercoaster of emotions she went through. Leah develops a practical and pastoral theology through wrestling with God, holding out for a blessing in the wilderness, even if that blessing is not the answered prayer she most desired.

She learns not to mask her real emotions of loss: anger, heartache, abandonment, empty, trauma, feeling unloved and abandoned. She had to give herself permission to feel the pain. She recognizes that in the trauma of grief you never feel yourself again, you must be remade and be patient in that remaking.

The book is an act of sacred, sacramental remembering, so that her beautiful son Reuben, gifted to her by God, will never be forgotten. It is also the hard lesson of learning to share her grief with the right people. That as people respond in uncaring and unhelpful ways, she can forgive but doesn't need to stay in those unhelpful relationships. Her experience has led her to deeply desire to build others up, not pull them down.

As I read the book, I sense she has been through a refining fire, her words have a purified resonance, that I think will help others who have experienced a loss that is literally unspeakable.

Leah has truly inhabited the in-between place between grief and hope with grace and truth and articulates how to hold on in that liminal space in a way that will enable others to grieve and heal without ever forgetting.

Revd Dr Shaun Lambert
Dip. Psych. Couns.; MA Integ. Couns. & Psychotherapy, Psychotherapist, Mindfulness Researcher, Author of Mindful Formation And Putting on the Wakeful one

Endorsements

'Having known Leah for many years personally, it has been a joy to sit and read Living In between Grief and Hope. Leah's journey has been one of love, suffering and sorrow, and it is laid bare in her writings alongside her search for hope in the midst of great tragedy.

As you read, you find yourself connecting with your own stories of loss, grief and sorrow which will bring healing emotionally and restore faith to our hearts where we may have lost. Leah is a creative communicator and writer who gently threads the needle and sews the broken fragments back together.'

Alison Fenning,
Founder of 'Mission on the Move' and Author of 'Lift Up Your Head'.

Leah has truly inhabited the in-between place between grief and hope with grace and truth and articulates how to hold on in that liminal space in a way that will enable others to grieve and heal without ever forgetting.

Revd Dr Shaun Lambert
Dip. Psych. Couns.; MA Integ. Couns. & Psychotherapy, Author, Psychotherapist, Mindfulness Researcher

Most of us experience loss and grief and struggle to know how to process it. Leah, through her own story, offers a compassionate invitation to walk that journey with her. Unafraid to articulate her pain, confusion and isolation, she faces them with honesty without allowing them to define her. Although my own experience is vastly different, I have been impacted by her wise reflections, finding myself pausing frequently to contemplate painful losses with fresh, healing insight. Ultimately this is a book brimming with hope as Leah discovers that Jesus is so close to the brokenhearted, and with tenderness and compassion he is able to hold us and our burdens while we regain our strength.

Claire Lambert
Author of The Returning King: Is God Preparing

Leah's courage and passion shines through this book. She has told her story so bravely, allowing the reader into her moments of intense vulnerability and pain, and it is from there that she offers true comfort, encouragement, and hope.

Liza Hoeksma
Book editor, life coach and author and co-author of many books including several with kintsugi hope.

Leah's life is a powerful testament to faith, resilience, and hope. Her steadfast trust in God through life's toughest moments is profoundly uplifting, and will illuminate your heart as you turn each page. Praise God for Leah's courage in sharing her story with the world.

Tom Smith
Worship Pastor at Soul survivor Watford

A Note to the Reader

Woven upon these pages are stories of numerous broken and desperate individuals, including my own. We learn that although hope may seem lost, it can be found within the depths of God's truth. While this book accompanies you in your pain, it also extends an invitation to live your life close to Jesus and to embrace hope by leading with love in a broken and fragile world. Our pain has the power to extend beyond ourselves, bringing hope into the lives of others.

Divided into five sections: 'Living, Learning, Longing, Leaning, and Leading,' each section represents the intricate journey of grief, where hope is discovered within the messy reality of brokenness, death, and life's fragility.

I used to believe grief was stealing my most precious moments. I used to fear time and chase happiness. I was made to believe that grief had no place in my life. Then I realized that if I didn't make space for sadness, I would never really know true joy. When we learn to walk with both grief and hope whilst giving them equal moments, we find joy again. We must remind ourselves that grief is remembering how much we loved someone, and spending time on love is never a waste of time; it's a gift.

I don't pretend to have all the answers, but I do desire to walk with you through your heartache with the power of words. I am open and vulnerable because I believe we all deserve to be restored and understood. Every loss and every grieving process is unique, and my aim is to make a space where you can find inner healing but also a place to embrace all your emotions, even if it isn't pretty.

SECTION ONE

LIVING THROUGH LOSS

CHAPTER 1

Waiting Room

The unknown is what is so frustrating about the waiting game. In hide and seek, while waiting, you're consumed by the thought of being found. When a TV series isn't clear on where it's heading, the fast-forward button then becomes a best friend. The truth is, I love a happy ending, and it's not my favourite thing to see something going wrong. I find myself shouting at the screen and then fast-forwarding to a better part in the series. If there is an option to opt-out of waiting, I will take it. I get so caught up in arriving at the happy ending that I forget the purpose of the journey. If we are honest with ourselves, a fast-paced life is attractive. It removes the frustration of having to wait, but sadly, there isn't a fast-forward button on our lives. Lady Mary Currie coined a classic saying: 'All things come to those who wait'. I would beg to differ; it could be true if you're sure what you're waiting for, but there are no bios or introductions to our life stories. There's always a chance we don't get what we hoped for, and that can damage our trust in waiting. Waiting takes a little courage, as nothing is really certain. But I've discovered another truth along the way, and this is that God will be good to us even if we are disappointed with the end result.

I had just had my 12-week scan. The sonographer sent me to a waiting room so the doctors could explain what was happening with my baby. With every door that slammed shut, and with every sound of moving feet, my heart would race so fast I felt I was going to faint. I was so anxious to know why I had been sent to the waiting room. I felt relieved when the silence in the room stopped, but I did not want to hear the words that filled the space. The midwife explained that my baby would not survive 16 weeks. They had sadly found fluid around the baby's neck. The thought of miscarrying made me physically ill. I was devastated. At that moment, it was the worst possible outcome after waiting 12 weeks with excitement to see my baby on the screen. I was being told my dream of being a mum of two wasn't possible right now. I wanted to go home with a scan of my baby and celebrate new life. Instead, I was going home with uncertainty.

I want to tell you a story about a group of people who had to wait a very long time to be rescued from their suffering. They were called the Israelites. A prideful king kept them as slaves, killed their children, and beat their people. The Israelites knew what it felt like to live through loss and endless waiting until, one day, a man of God called Moses was sent by God to free them. After a long wait, Moses succeeded, and their waiting came to an end. But, as they walked into freedom, they entered another challenge. Moses was leading them to what they called the Promised Land. However, it took them 40 years to arrive. God purposefully took them the long way because He knew that when things got hard they would just give up [1].

When I heard my baby's diagnosis, I entered a waiting period that I didn't have the strength to enter. But there was no option to fast forward this time. I found that I needed to be still, be present, and know that there is a God who will fight for me. That same truth and promise is also for you. Pregnancy often feels like the long way round to the promised land. God is so powerful that He could just grow our babies overnight, so why doesn't He? Why do we have to wait without the power to do anything about it? God made the Israelites wait, not for His benefit or because He wanted them to suffer even more, but for their own good. God knew they would change their minds and turn back. By making them wait, He was teaching the Israelites to trust in Him and not in their own ability to walk the path of waiting; to trust God to fight for them when things got hard. While we wait, we can choose to trust and believe that God is for us and not against us, or we can change our minds and turn away from trusting God to trusting in our own ability. While we wait, we can believe that "Good things come to those who wait" [2]. God will show His compassion to the broken-hearted and will give strength to those who are weary.

A lot about waiting is frustrating because of the fear of wasting time and losing out. I desperately wanted a big family and I didn't want to have to go through loss. I didn't want to have to wait and see if my pregnancy was going to work. I feel ashamed even admitting this fact because it's just not true that we lose out. We don't lose time for going through suffering. We gain much more than we can imagine. It is perfectly explained in Romans, which tells us that 'waiting does not diminish us, any more than waiting diminishes a pregnant mother' [3]. We are enlarged in the waiting. We, of course, don't know what is enlarging us. But the longer we wait, the larger we become, and the more joyful our expectancy. Meanwhile, the moment we get tired in the waiting, God's spirit is right alongside us helping us along. If we don't know how or what to pray, it doesn't matter. He does our praying in and for us, making prayer out of our wordless sighs, our aching groans [4]. He knows us far better than we know ourselves, He knows our longing, and keeps us present before God. That's why we can be sure that every detail in our love for God is worked into something good.

I don't know where you are right now, but I know I was tired of waiting. I was fearful of the loss that was before me. The only way to be enlarged in the waiting is to remove the fear of the stillness and to choose to be fully present, because when we are still, God can move even more in our lives. There's a part of the story I was telling about the Israelites in which they come across a barrier during their long walk to the promised land. That barrier was called the Red Sea. The king decided he no longer wanted them to be free and was chasing after them. The Israelites had to wait for a miracle as they stood before a huge barrier to their freedom. Then God parted the sea so the Israelites could walk freely into the promised land. I can imagine the Israelites in that moment while they were waiting for something to happen while feeling like nothing would. They probably thought that was the end. However, God made a way and enlarged their hope in Him. It also says in Romans 8 that the more we wait, the more joyful our expectancy becomes. This doesn't mean expecting that all will be fine. The Israelites didn't get to avoid their barrier. They still walked through the Red Sea. Walking through a parted sea must have been terrifying. When I left the hospital that day with the dreadful report, I was entering into a season where I would have to choose faith in the waiting, and my hope was enlarged. Not because things were going to be great, but because I was waiting on God, who I had faith in. We may not all have a Red Sea moment, but with enough hope to take the next step or pray the next prayer, God will hear your cries, just like He heard the cries of the Israelites.

I want to remind you of the quote I used at the beginning of the chapter: 'All things come to those who wait.' The question I asked myself, and I want to ask you, is: what and who are you waiting on? I learned quickly that waiting on a miracle wasn't the answer. I had to make the decision not to wait on receiving what I had prayed for, but to wait on Jesus alone. When we wait on Jesus and we are expectant on who God says He is, God is good, because that's who He is. But this doesn't mean we must give up hoping for the miracle of healing. I believe God heals today. Charles Spurgeon said, 'Those who do not hope cannot wait; but if we hope for that we see not, then do we with patience wait for it.'

References:

[1] Exodus 13:17-18 (NIV): 'It so happened that after Pharaoh released the people, God didn't lead them by the road through the land of the Philistines, which was the shortest route, for God thought, "If the people encounter war, they'll change their minds and go back to Egypt." So God led the people on the wilderness road, looping around to the Red Sea. The Israelites left Egypt in military formation.'

[2] James 5:7-11 (NIV): 'Be patient, then, brothers and sisters, until the Lord's coming. See how the farmer waits for the land to yield its valuable crop, patiently waiting for the autumn and spring rains. You too, be patient and stand firm, because the Lord's coming is near. Don't grumble against one another, brothers and sisters, or you will be judged. The Judge is standing at the door! Brothers and sisters, as an example of patience in the face of suffering, take the prophets who spoke in the name of the Lord. As you know, we count as blessed those who have persevered. You have heard of Job's perseverance and have seen what the Lord finally brought about. The Lord is full of compassion and mercy.'

[3] Romans 8:24-26 (NIV)

[4] Romans 8:26 (NIV)

CHAPTER 2

Chasing Hope

I had never been so desperate for a miracle to take place. I wanted it so badly, and everything within me didn't want to let go of hope. While I was busy waiting for my next appointments and attending check-ups every two weeks, it almost felt like my life was running ahead of me. We had finally got to the 16-week scan, and it felt like I had arrived on dry land after walking through my own Red Sea, holding onto hope through uncertainty. The doctor said in his own words that a miracle had taken place and that the fluid had left my baby's neck! This meant that my son had a chance to live and be a part of our family.

We celebrated the gift of healing and celebrated a new milestone. I could finally breathe. Trouble had left my side, and I could enjoy the journey of my pregnancy. I finally felt I had an explanation for all the unanswered prayers and disappointment. God surely wanted to bring hope to those who were waiting for a miracle, and my story would ignite faith and hope. But little did I know what was to come next!

I had a month of living on a high before it became a crashing low. The same was true for the Israelites after they walked through the parted sea and then realised that they had more food when they were slaves. They didn't think the journey was worth it anymore. I could relate! After a month of living with a miracle, I lay on another hospital bed waiting for the gender reveal. Instead of experiencing a moment of joy, I was entirely heartbroken when they told me that my baby boy had only a 1% chance of survival. Tragically, they could see a few abnormalities that could result in his death. They couldn't offer me many options other than waiting it out or having a termination.

Holding on to the 1% reminded me of a parable taught to us in Matthew 18. Shepherds who tend to their sheep are serious about looking after every one of them wholeheartedly. In this story, there were one hundred sheep altogether, and one poor sheep went missing. The shepherd decided to leave all ninety-nine to look for the one that was lost. The parable of the lost sheep teaches us that every person is worth fighting for, but it also teaches us that there is hope. There is hope in chasing after what seems like a lost cause. Jesus says that when you seek him, you will find him [5]. It's not hope in a miracle that we need to chase—it's hope in Jesus that we need to chase, because it's in him that we have hope.

The good news in this story is that Jesus is the good shepherd, and that he is the one doing the finding. God had to work hard with the Israelites as they prayed from a place of disappointment time and time again. He never failed to provide for them or guide them like a good shepherd. God never gets tired or weary as we do. He's working overtime, and there's nothing you can do to separate yourself from His love or hope.

To pick up where we left off with the Israelites, we find them approaching the land they had walked so hard to get to. Like them, I was approaching the end of my pregnancy journey. I was nearly at the end of my pregnancy, and my baby had grown to the size of a bell pepper. I could nearly imagine what life would be like once he was outside of the womb. At 16 weeks, I had such a breakthrough, and just like that, it was taken from me with endless bad reports. I was repeatedly told the risks involved if I decided to continue with my pregnancy, such as the risk of my baby dying in the womb or the risk of sudden labour that would result in prematurity.

The Israelites wandered in the wilderness for forty years because they believed the bad reports about the land they desired to live in. I am not going to lie, the bad reports the doctors gave me scared me so much that, at some points, I wanted to give up. However, the hope within me wouldn't let the bad reports be my only truth. Whatever the bad report may be, it doesn't change the truth we know about our God. We can still hold to the fact that our God is a healer and is our ultimate hope. So that's what I did! In the end, Moses was fearful and gave up, so God sent two different people into the land: Joshua and Caleb. Sadly, Moses never got to see the Promised Land because he chose to believe the bad reports that scared him into giving up. He lived on the outside of the promise for the rest of his life. Joshua and Caleb brought back a good report from the same land. The difference is that they chose to see what God had promised and not what scared them the most. Some of you may be living in a wilderness longer than you need to because you have believed the lies that there's nothing good to trust anymore. Some of you believe there is no hope and you're about to give up. I encourage you to reach out to Jesus. That is where you will not fail to find hope. Others of you have a lack of vision. God wants you to reach out for the hope he offers so freely; the hope for comfort and the hope that there is a future beyond your bad report. One of my favourite quotes comes from Anne Frank, who saw immeasurable suffering during the Holocaust. She said, 'Where there is hope, there is life.' What a gift to hold on to even the darkest days!

References:

[5] Matthew 7:7 (NIV): 'Ask and it will be given to you; seek and you will find; knock and the door will be opened to you.'

CHAPTER 3

——————

A Promise

Nothing can beat the feeling of arriving somewhere when you have been waiting so long to get there. I remember when we finally arrived at the delivery date. We had waited nearly nine months, nine months that had been a rollercoaster of emotions. The professionals never expected us to get as far as full term, and everyone was anxious to see the outcome. I was terrified to get to the end of the pregnancy, as it meant I would have to face so much that I didn't think I had the strength to get through. I was afraid of the worst outcome and that my hope in God would be put to shame.

It was the day before New Year's Eve that they decided to medically intervene because my labour wasn't progressing. They gave me a caesarean section. Within minutes, my baby boy Reuben Josiah was out of my womb, and his eyes were gazing into mine. That moment was one to be remembered. He was a living, breathing miracle.

I want to take this moment to acknowledge that not everyone arrives at this point. Maybe you're reading this, and you're thinking about how you didn't get to see your baby face-to-face or about how you didn't get to see a miracle in answer to your prayers for a loved one. I want to say that God doesn't love you any less just because your prayer wasn't answered or because your expectations weren't met. Jesus loved his mum, yet even she had to go through the pain of losing him and seeing him die a brutal death. The end result of a period of waiting isn't dependent on how faithful we have been or how well we have prayed. God promises that He will never leave us or forsake us, and that will never change regardless of the result.

I held onto the promise that I wasn't alone, and that God was with me. Each day I would visit baby Reuben in the NICU. He was given oxygen to help him breathe, and he looked quite pink and plump as a baby should. Sadly, I still didn't truly know how unwell he was, and we were still waiting on blood results. So, I made the most of being with him and held his tiny hands while I would gently speak to him. Every day I wrote him a letter. On the front of each letter, I would write in bold, colourful letters a promise of God for his life.

On the first day of his life, the promise I chose was inspired by Isaiah 43: 'He who formed you, fear not, for I have redeemed you; I have called you by name, and you are mine, and I am the Lord your God.'[6] As fear gripped me, these words were like water to a dry throat. Ultimately, God knows our names. We are His priority. Just like the shepherd going after the lost sheep that we talked about in Chapter 2, each one of us is God's number one child; He will drop everything to get to know us. God has redeemed us; His love dissolves our fear. God is our Father and he promises to fight for us. We have a purpose. God formed us, and there is a reason for the existence of every human being. Living matters to God, you matter to God, and the people you love matter to God. We don't just 'belong' to God; He loves us so very much, like a father loves his children. God loves us so much that he sent his son Jesus to die a brutal death so that we could know his grace and mercy. The day I wrote this letter, a fight for life rose within me. I wasn't going to stop believing for a miracle. I would wake up every few hours to express my milk, and then I would walk to the ward to give Reuben his feed. I remember how painful it was to move after a C-section, but I pushed past the pain to provide for his needs. God is our Father, and He will fight for us. He experiences all the suffering we go through with us.

Carrying the promises of God daily and writing a new one daily was a way for me to survive; I needed it for the weeks ahead. I spent three of the first days on my own in the aftercare ward, and my husband went home to look after our little boy, who was only two at the time. It was tough for all of us.

The fourth day changed everything. We had an appointment with the many doctors who were helping to keep Reuben alive using various machines. My husband Judah had visited that day with our son, Elijah—so, thankfully, I wasn't alone in the meeting. Elijah was restless in this small side room, and I was once again anxious to hear the blood test results that would determine our next steps.

Our lovely doctor had so much compassion. He sat so still as he told us the news that would shatter our hearts. I didn't prepare myself for more disappointment, and so I was in shock when he told us that Reuben had a chromosome disorder called Trisomy 18 that was incompatible with life. I had written a promise card just that morning that read, 'Then you will have healing for your body and strength for your bones' (Proverbs) [7]. Hope isn't always found when we're focused on what we want, but it is found in Jesus, and that's who I went to.

The hours passed so quickly. Suddenly, it was the seventh day, and we were being given a room to be with Reuben. We played soft worship music and held our boy with the hope that we would see him live another day. It was late, and I was enjoying being together as a family. I started to picture what it would be like to go home together. For a moment, things felt quite normal as I sent Judah to get some more baby grows. While he was gone, I was watching Reuben and noticed he was struggling to breathe, so I called the doctor. This had happened before, and I was expecting a medical check and some more oxygen. The room was still, and the doctor said with a soft voice, 'It's time'. I thought I had missed something. Time for what? Medicine? Oxygen? He told me that Reuben was dying. Words cannot describe the pain I was feeling. I felt like I was dying. Around the same time the doctor was telling me what was happening, Judah's mum had called him with a vision of Reuben in the arms of Jesus. By the time I phoned him, he was already on his way back to be with us.

We entered into another time of waiting, but this time, it wasn't for healing. It was for Jesus to take my little boy to heaven. That morning, I asked Judah if he would like to write a promise for Reuben. Judah wrote a promise inspired by Deuteronomy 31:6: 'Be strong and courageous, don't be afraid, for the Lord your God is with you.' God said this to Joshua when he entered the Promised Land and had more battles to face. On the back of the promise note, Judah had written a few words to Reuben. He said, 'Every breath you make and every moment lived is taken with your heavenly Father as he holds you in his arms, full of love, life, and peace. He will never leave you or forsake you, Reuben. This is a promise.'

This promise card wasn't just for Reuben that day; it was God speaking to us. God is so kind that He would prepare us for our trial with His words of hope, even though we couldn't see any reason to hope with our natural eyes. Hope was placed as a gift in a promise card, and I believe it was placed there for you to hear those words too. Be strong and courageous, God is with you! You are not going through whatever is ahead alone. Like Joshua entering a promised land with battles still to face, I had a few battles ahead of me.

The night was closing in, and we entered another day with Reuben still peacefully breathing. The words from a worship song which says, '...worthy of every breath we could ever breathe, we live for you...' were playing in the background as we lay with Reuben. God was so perfectly with us, even if we didn't fully feel it. It was like I felt as if a city was between me and God. I couldn't feel Him, let alone hear Him. I just knew He was there by faith. I just decided to believe there was hope; I knew I needed it to survive. My experience with hope wasn't a highly spiritual moment; it involved a choice that I made through gritted teeth. I cried so much that my eyes started to feel heavy while my husband stayed awake holding Reuben, and I fell asleep. I woke up sharply, and I believe it was the Holy Spirit waking me. I took Reuben out of Judah's hands and cradled him to sleep for the last time. Before he took his last breath, he looked at me one last time. The room was filled with grief as I held my breathless baby boy, still clutching to hope. I bathed him for the first and last time before laying him to rest with the seven promise notes we had written him.

The promises of God are not always about arriving at a destination like the Promised Land, as was the case for the Israelites. God's promises can walk you through the journey of loss. They have gone before you, and they are working in your life right now. When it comes to trusting someone to catch you when you're falling, you'll be scared when you fall. But sometimes, trusting is your only choice for survival. The truth is, we will never really arrive at the ultimate destination or find the answers to our questions until we meet Jesus face-to-face. Suffering will be forever knit into our being, but it will always be alongside God's hope, which is woven within the depths of our agony.

References:

[6] Isaiah 43:1 (ESV): 'But now thus says the LORD, he who created you, O Jacob, he who formed you, O Israel: "Fear not, for I have redeemed you; I have called you by name, you are mine.'

[7] Proverbs 3:8 (NLT): 'Then you will have healing for your body and strength for your bones.'

CHAPTER 4

The Empty Tomb

Walking out of the NICU ward with empty arms was the bravest walk I had ever done. I felt disconnected from my body as I watched those leaving the same hospital with healthy newborns. What grieved me the most was that no one knew that I had just had a baby, even though I felt the emptiness in my arms where I once held my precious boy. My body was still recovering from labour and a caesarean. My breasts continued to produce milk and begged for a baby to feed. I felt so empty, and these words of Job could have been mine: 'I am given months of emptiness and miserable nights' [8].

In the following months, I would have vivid dreams that I was holding Reuben. I would wake up drenched in sweat with tears running down my face, searching for Reuben in a panic. Each time the emptiness would hit me afresh. It was like he had just died again. Grief was ripping a huge hole in my heart as I came to terms with the fact that I would never hold him or have him lie on my chest.

The reminders of those who have gone cause such emptiness in our daily lives. No earthly thing can really fill it. It can cause us to lose our appetite for food, take our sleep away from us, and take the desire to have fun and know joy. My relationships with people and God felt empty—like they had no real meaning or purpose anymore. I was running on zero fuel but still managed to mask being okay and come across as if I had an overflowing tank of grace and love. The truth is I didn't really want people to see how much I was suffering. My loss felt private and vulnerable, and I was scared I would be damaged even more. My mask was a way of protecting myself from those who, in my opinion, weren't equipped to deal with my grief. I often received awkward comments from those who just wanted to help but couldn't. I honestly felt more alone after I shared how I felt. For a while, masking my feelings was how I coped, but I knew it couldn't be that way forever.

By the time the day to bury Reuben came, I was still great at pretending to be faith-filled despite losing a loved one. It was like my real emotions were locked inside the same grave that Reuben was buried in—and for a time, they were. The sad thing about masking your true feelings is that it doesn't change how empty you feel. Every day I felt lonely and, if I am honest, I found it hard to carry on living. But hope would always tug me away from my frightening thoughts.

I will speak more about the emotions of grief in the next section (Learning to Grieve), but first, I want to look at a story that helped me unlock my emptiness.

The story is from the Gospel of John, where we read that Jesus was placed in a tomb after his death on the cross, where he died for our sins. He was in the tomb for three days. Mary Magdalene, who was one of Jesus' committed followers, went to the tomb and saw that the stone had been removed from the entrance. So, she came running to Simon Peter and the other disciple, the one Jesus loved, and said, "They have taken the Lord out of the tomb, and we don't know where they have put him!" [9]

The tomb is an important part of the story. The stone that held Jesus inside the tomb, which was then rolled away, represents life after death. Matthew 28:2 reads: 'And behold, there was a great earthquake, for an angel of the Lord descended from heaven and came and rolled back the stone, and sat upon it' [10]. As seen in John, Mary, in her grief, became distressed and started to weep when she saw that Jesus was no longer there. A man she thought was the gardener approached her. In fact, it was Jesus, and he asked her why she was crying. Mary replies, "They have taken my Lord away" [11]. In response, Jesus simply says her name— "Mary"—and at that moment, she recognises who is standing beside her [12].

I took two lessons from this story which intrigued me. Firstly, for the emptiness of the tomb to be seen, the stone had to be rolled away. This emptiness for me represented my disappointment in Jesus. I was disappointed because I felt abandoned and unloved. It wasn't that I didn't believe anymore. Rather, I was hurt, and this made me put a few walls up. The stones that make up these walls that we put up can be heavy, and that's because we want to protect ourselves. But what Mary didn't know in her weeping was that Jesus was beside her the whole time—she just couldn't see him for who he was. It wasn't until he said her name that she recognised who he was. In all the emptiness I was feeling, I started to realise that I still had a name: an identity separate from the emptiness that I felt, even though it didn't feel like that at the time.

The second lesson that I learned is that the walls I was putting up were stopping me from having a full relationship with Jesus. Without the stone rolling away that day at the tomb of Jesus, we wouldn't be able to have a relationship with the Father. Jesus wants to enter our empty spaces, spaces where we feel heartbroken, angry, and disappointed with Him. He wants to fill us with His love. I found that by shutting Jesus out, I was also shutting out his love. More fear was creeping into my everyday life, and in the end, I felt more empty. In the end, I realised that I hadn't been abandoned by Jesus. Rather, I was rejecting his love because I was angry with him.

There are times in my emptiness that I felt I didn't know where my saviour was. But God was patient with me. He shouted my name until I heard it and remembered who He really was. As for you, I know that Jesus is shouting your name; he wants you to let him in wherever it hurts the most. God will not allow us to be left empty even when our loss is so tangible that it feels like He has.

I want to take us back to the story of the Israelites. When they left Egypt, they didn't leave empty-handed even though they had lost so much physically. I mentioned in the first chapter that Pharaoh had chosen to kill the Israelites' first-born children. So, we know they had suffered a devastating loss. The Israelites also lost their homes and freedom as slaves under Pharaoh. The day the Israelites left Egypt, God told them to gather all the finest jewels from the land for the journey. Although their jewels were physical, spiritually, God leaves us with gifts when we give him our emptiness. Isaiah 61 says, 'To all who mourn in Israel, he will give a crown of beauty for ashes, a joyous blessing instead of mourning, festive praise instead of despair. In their righteousness, they will be like great oaks that the LORD has planted for his own glory' [13].

One afternoon, I was sitting on my couch, looking out the window, and crying out, 'Why me? Why did I have to lose my baby?' Jesus spoke to me and said, 'You never lost Reuben. I gave him to you as a gift.' I was stunned. My perspective had to change—just as it did for Mary after she cried out for Jesus. She feared that she had lost him, but Jesus reminded her that he was never lost. He was always beside her. She just didn't recognise him. The gift of Reuben to me was still very much alive and would stay with me for the rest of my days. Loved ones that have gone too soon will always be a gift, even if they're not with you physically. The treasured memories, favourite books, and cuddly toys will remind you of who they were. The gift of life is irreversible. Love for those who have been given to us grows deeper by the day, and no one can take that gift of love away.

In the following chapters, I will take you on a journey to show you how God will turn your ashes into beauty and your mourning into joy. Queen Elizabeth II said after WW2 had ended that 'grief is the price we pay for love.'

References:

[8] Job 7:3 (NIV): 'I am given months of emptiness, and nights of misery have been allotted to me.'

[9] John 20:1-2 (NIV): 'Early on the first day of the week, while it was still dark, Mary Magdalene went to the tomb and saw that the stone had been removed from the entrance. So she came running to Simon Peter and the other disciple, the one Jesus loved, and said, "They have taken the Lord out of the tomb, and we don't know where they have put him!"'

[10] Matthew 28:2 (MSG): 'Suddenly the earth reeled and rocked under their feet as God's angel came down from heaven, came right up to where they were standing. He rolled back the stone and then sat on it.'

[11] John 20:13 (NLT): 'Dear woman, why are you crying?' the angels asked her. 'Because they have taken away my Lord,' she replied, 'and I don't know where they have put him.'

[12] John 20:16 (NLT): 'Mary!' Jesus said. She turned to him and cried out, 'Rabboni!' (which is Hebrew for 'Teacher').'

[13] Isaiah 61:3 (NLT): 'To all who mourn in Israel, he will give a crown of beauty for ashes, a joyous blessing instead of mourning, festive praise instead of despair. In their righteousness, they will be like great oaks that the LORD has planted for his own glory.'

SECTION 2

LEARNING TO GRIEVE

CHAPTER 5

A Space to Heal

Grief is, in my experience, complex. There isn't a formula that helps us learn to grieve, and there isn't a perfect step-by-step guide to healing. For me, learning to grieve was about giving myself permission to feel the pain and space to find healing. I know healing isn't simple and is incredibly painful. That's why it's important for me to tell you that there is a place for your grief. In this chapter, I want to encourage you by telling you that there is a place prepared for you to grieve in your suffering and during your wandering in the wilderness. God's desire is to nourish your broken heart.

I think of times when I would sit around a table to eat with family or friends. I would feel like the odd one out, like I really didn't belong there. My pain seemed too deep, and my thoughts too much, for others to handle. I could see people looking at me, and I could hear their silence. I wanted someone to acknowledge my suffering and pain; maybe then I would feel a part of this world again. Vincent van Gogh has a famous painting of an empty chair, called 'Van Gogh's Chair'. It felt like an expression of how I was feeling, and it gave me comfort. The chair's emptiness intrigued me. It seemed to be screaming to be sat on, to be experienced. As I stared at the painting, I sensed that God was pushing me to fully experience what it felt like to sit on the chair of grief. God wanted me to know that there was a safe place for me to heal; that although grief had been a scary and tormenting place, it would soon be a place where I would experience healing.

Grief can sometimes make you feel like all your comfort is being removed. When you replace an old, worn chair you have been sitting on for years with a new chair, it feels uncomfortable for a while, and it takes a while to break in. It is the same with our grief. But we are not alone. I hope that as I share my story, you will begin to feel like I have been sitting in your new chair of grief and made it slightly warm so that when you come to sit down to grieve, it will ease some of the discomfort.

The Bible tells us of a vision about a pregnant woman in labour and a dragon waiting to kill her child. God swoops in to save her child just in time and takes the boy to heaven. Revelation 12:7 then tells us that the woman fled into the wilderness, where God had prepared a place to care for her for 1,260 days. Then, there was war in heaven. Michael, an archangel, and his angels fought against the dragon and his angels. The dragon lost the battle, and he and his angels were forced out of heaven.

This story doesn't just remind us that God has victory over death and that Satan will not win the war surrounding our grief, but it also reminds us there is a place for us to grieve. In that place of grieving, God wants to take care of us. Additionally, we see that God doesn't want us to be afraid of the wilderness. The wilderness is a barren land. It's empty and unattractive. But throughout scripture, we are told it's a place of growth. It's where Jesus was both tested and nourished by God.

In Revelation 12:6, the woman had to run into the wilderness for her safety. This would have been unbearable, as she was running to save her life and her child's life. Grief can feel like labour pains, and in every moment of grief the enemy is trying to take away whatever is left of your endurance and hope. To survive, we also have to run freely into the wilderness in order to be nourished by God. This looks like allowing yourself to feel the pain and loss that you are experiencing while letting

Jesus run with you. While you may be running from the wilderness, God is calling you into it. There's a hidden beauty to be found in the places we most fear.

A wave of 'contractions' will come time and time again, stabbing you, preparing you, and stretching you for new life. I went through seasons of feeling like I belonged and seasons in which I found peace in my loss. Then, the strong waves of grief would come again. Restless nights would keep me awake again. There are times when we can be fully confident that there's a time and place in which we will know peace. Though the stillness of the wilderness can scare you, I encourage you to embrace both the grief and the moments of hope. What can feel like a rollercoaster of emotions can coincide with letting go and drawing closer to Jesus. I remember when I would go for drives in the evenings alone just so I could cry out in my pain. I wouldn't always pray, but God was always there with me. His presence often felt like peace or simply just the security I needed to be real.

I am not saying that embracing hope in grief is about finding a physical place to sit in order to grieve. Rather, I am saying that it is about finding your place in the world while healing. I remember the feeling of being detached from the world. It was like something was always missing, and I cannot really say that I found the missing piece to the puzzle. The truth is, when you have experienced the trauma of loss, you never feel like 'you' again. So, maybe finding your place is about being confident enough to be the new 'you' that knows suffering, and then about finding the courage to be taken care of.

Nourishment

In another translation of the Bible, the word 'nourishment' is used in places where God speaks about taking care of us. 'Nourishment' communicates the kind of care you'd show a child that needs feeding, or a flower that needs water. Nourishment, then, can lead to growth. When a seed is nourished with water, it soon sprouts out of the darkness of the soil and becomes what it was destined to be. God will do all He can to bring growth into your wilderness. When I think of my growth in my wilderness, much of it was about learning to be patient. To be honest, I didn't really have a lot of choice but to wait. So, without my asking, my ability to have patience grew stronger. There was a time after Reuben passed in which I could only think about having another baby. Each 28-day cycle became something endured. After half a year of trying, I became impatient. Sadly, since Reuben, we have lost another child through a miscarriage. Patience has taught my heart to be still in times of despair and heartbreak. Life can feel like a long waiting room in which we wait for healing, answered prayer, and changing seasons. The area you grow in may be completely different to mine, but I encourage you to lean in to the nourishment.

In my experience, growth can feel like the last stages of labour; the stages in which you push, although nothing seems to be happening. Until, suddenly, you have given birth. Then it's all happening. Pushing is the stage of labour in which pain is at its height. All the while, you're required to fully concentrate on giving birth. The focus is on persevering so that you can reach the goal. Romans 5:3-5 tells us that, ultimately, our perseverance will produce HOPE. When we push past trials towards Jesus, hope will be produced. What I love about labour—and there's not much—is the gentle but firm voice of the midwife telling me when it's the right time to push. She'd always tell me when I'd start contracting, which is the most painful part of the labour. In those most painful moments, the midwife was there to guide and direct me so that the baby would safely arrive. Similarly, when we listen to the voice of

Jesus, we receive the wisdom which tells us when to push and when to wait. You are not alone in your pushing. God will guide you. I would say I am currently in a season of 'pushing' as I persevere towards healing. Since losing Reuben, my confidence has come down like a deflating balloon. Building that back up is exhausting. My mind likes to play tricks with me and bullies me into thinking that I am unloved and rejected. The push can feel like a fight. We have no strength to fight, but our God fights for us with His care and love.

When we are pushing through to find a place to grieve, we need to be aware that Satan doesn't want us to survive. But, just as God prepared a place for the woman to heal, he will also take care of you and prepare a place for you. He will take care of you and prepare a place for you to heal. I like this image of God preparing a spacious place to heal and to be loved. We live in a world that wants to move on so quickly that you can feel forced to try and heal as quickly as possible.

To be nourished also means to be fed or to be fattened. Looking at what we are eating from a spiritual perspective is important. We are told by Jesus that we cannot eat bread alone to survive. Reading the Bible became a way of feeding my spirit and healing a broken heart. I kept it simple. Just reading a Psalm a day and spending some time meditating on it was helpful. The Psalms are so helpful because they are filled with lament; with real-life prayers. While people were telling me to smile more, God was teaching me how to grieve healthily. That meant being true to where I was, with a hope that one day I would find joy again.

God has gone before you to prepare a place for you to be nourished and loved. I would like to encourage you to invite Jesus to care for you.

CHAPTER 6

Sacred Tears

When you live in-between grief and hope, tears are a regular visitor. If you're like me, crying is a vulnerable activity that leaves you feeling bruised and fragile. Tears leave a mark—not just physically, but mentally. I would look in the mirror after a silent cry, and I would be bloodshot. I would be physically and mentally tired after feeling shame and anger all throughout the night while I cried. I'll admit that I like a good old cry because afterwards, I feel like something has been released from me. But, I hate crying in front of people. So, when I cried, I would feel incredibly alone. Reading the words of David brought me much comfort—particularly those from Psalm 56: 'You've kept track of my every toss and turn, through the sleepless nights, Each tear entered in your ledger, each ache written in your book' [14].

Every sleepless night and every tear is stored up by Jesus, who makes a note of each and everything. Your tears are welcome and remembered. I believe our tears are sacred because they connect us with our Father God. Whereas we sometimes find ourselves trying to hide them because we feel they are not socially acceptable, each tear is noted and known by God. I think back to the early days of being a mum. Every time I heard that newborn cry, I would fly out of my skin to attend to the needs of the baby. I would know what each cry meant, whether that be a request for food, more sleep, or entertainment. I would take note of my children's needs so that as they grew up, I would know what kind of response they needed from me. Just imagine how much more the Father takes notes of His children's weeping. The Bible tells us that God knows our every thought; that God knows everything about us. He cares and loves more fiercely than any human being ever could, ever.

Over the years, weeping is something I have become less shy about. I have learned to incorporate them into the way I live. Tears have a way of connecting you to the heart of God. I have seen this time and again. Allowing Jesus to heal me through being vulnerable has brought me closer to him. I am reassured that I am safe, accepted, and cared for. However, even though at times I have felt close to Jesus when I have been weeping, I can also feel like I am reaching out and yearning for something I can't have. The pain of this cuts deep.

There is a place in the Bible which refers to Jesus weeping gently as he was walking towards his friend's grave. He was just about to raise this friend—Lazarus—from the dead, but he had heard the cries of those who loved Lazarus, and this made Jesus weep. Jesus wept at the thought of Lazarus lying there dead and at the thought of his family mourning his death. Jesus knew there was more to the story, but he still wept. The point here is that Jesus sees the suffering, and he weeps with us—even though he knows that there's more after we die. Jesus doesn't expect us to be robotic and unmoved by the pain and suffering in the world. Weeping is a part of the process of healing. When we harden our hearts, we cannot weep, and then we cannot see healing because of the hardness we carry within. Jesus knows our loved ones are safe, happy, and cared for, but he chooses to respond to our suffering because he cares for us.

Holding back tears

There was once a time when I would hold back tears all day, every day. Letting go of my emotions was like a dam bursting. It would often come out in anger and would often result in something breaking. There is a lot of shame I have about the times I have had raging outbursts in front of my husband and children. Once, after we had just moved towns, I didn't want to cook, so we ordered some fish and chips. Bad idea! You see, we had moved from an area by the sea, where fresh fish was common, to the centre of Watford. I wasn't happy with the fish, which, having started on my plate, ended up being thrown across our new living room. I wasn't angry at my husband or the fish, but it was the day before Reuben's birthday. I hadn't given myself time to cry or to take in the emotion, so the poor fish and chips took the beating. It wasn't my proudest moment. I soon realised that the emotion which is held in will break out at some point.

In the Bible, there is a beautiful story about a woman who comes to Jesus and weeps at his feet while washing them with her tears. The expression of her sorrow was deeply intimate. She ultimately wanted forgiveness, but there is something wonderful here about the way she worships with her tears. This story can be an encouragement for us because it suggests that all the shame we feel about not being who we were before grief can just go away.

Before losing Reuben, my worship looked very joyful and passionate. Afterwards, it came out as either silent tears or loud cries when no one was around; it came out as the burying of my face into Reuben's red and white striped baby grow; it came out as grief—but I wasn't just crying into an empty space, I was crying with Jesus by my side. These sacred tears became my worship. I cried out to Jesus, and Jesus responded to every drop.

In Roman times, it was common to collect your tears of mourning when a person died, put them into a bottle, and put them in the grave with the deceased. I like this as a reminder to value my own tears and to give myself permission to weep. I don't collect my tears, but I intentionally take note of my feelings. Giving yourself permission to feel is the first step towards bursting the dam so that you can experience the feeling of being loved and of knowing that God acknowledges every tear that is shed.

References:

[14] Psalm 56:8 (MSG): 'You've kept track of my every toss and turn, through the sleepless nights, Each tear entered in your ledger, each ache written in your book.'

CHAPTER 7

Fragmented Hearts

When we have allowed ourselves to open up to the possibility of healing, we face the fragments of our brokenness. For me, this was gruelling and life-sucking, as it required attention and time. My grief felt like it had been magnified a thousand times. I would notice anger, pride, and selfishness appear through my pain. For example, I hadn't realised that I felt like I was a victim in every part of my life. I acted like everyone was to blame for the abandonment that I felt. Everywhere I went, I felt rejected, and I disliked anyone who would share their opinions about how I should heal. I was angry that I no longer felt needed now that I was fractured and broken. Of course, most of this was in my head, but it didn't change the reality of my rage. Grief can make you feel like you have been beaten up and left for dead.

God didn't leave me, and He won't leave you. There is a moment in the Bible in which thousands of people needed feeding. Jesus took a tiny lunch and miraculously made it stretch to feed the crowd. His disciples had been working hard and were worried they wouldn't have any food left for themselves. Jesus said, 'Gather the pieces that are left over. Let nothing be wasted' [15].

Let's pause for a moment and put ourselves in the shoes of the disciples. They surrendered everything to follow Jesus. They sacrificed food and sleep so Jesus could heal the sick. They all probably felt drained and desperate for food of their own, not whatever was left over. When you have been through a great loss, it can feel that nothing good is left over, and that all that remains are fragments of your heart. Listening to Jesus' words, I can imagine him speaking to us in our grief, saying: 'gather up the fragments and let nothing be wasted', because what's left is going to give you life and healing.

When a Jewish couple gets married, they traditionally break a glass by standing on it during the ceremony. The glass is wrapped up in a cloth for the sake of safety before they stand on it while shouting 'mazel tov'. It's a significant moment of symbolism. The broken glass symbolises the destruction of the Jewish temples, and it reminds the gathered people of the mourning that followed. Furthermore, they use glass because it can be moulded back together as a symbol of new life. There's beautiful poetry in the image of something being broken and then being given a new beginning through being moulded back together again. The fragments of our broken hearts can also be put back together if we find the courage to gather up what's left and give it to God. Living with both Jesus and loss can feel like a marriage. It's hard, messy, and there are many broken pieces. In any marriage, it is God that unifies the couple and makes them one. When we are unified with God, all of our brokenness is accepted. Because Jesus loves us, he gently puts the pieces back together.

Fragments are messy. As I've mentioned, during the Jewish wedding, the glass is wrapped up in a cloth to stop the pieces from flying all over the place. Jesus wants to be the cloth that holds our brokenness. What we don't want is to be pierced by the broken glass of our broken lives, flying in every direction. Sadly, for me, I was cut because I shared my grief with the wrong person and trusted the wrong crowd with my vulnerabilities. As a result, I wasn't taken care of as I deserved. We are precious to Jesus, and when we leave our broken mess in the wrong hands, it can cause damage. I am not saying that we shouldn't confide in anyone. There are people God has put in your life that you can trust to hold your broken heart. But, truthfully, Jesus is the only person who can deal with your broken pieces in the way you deserve.

The Aroma of What's Left

I have a memory box with all Reuben's things in it, such as the letters I wrote to him, his blankets, and his baby grows. These fragments of what's left of Reuben's life help me to connect with my memory of him. Every now and again, I will get them out. The smell of Reuben lingers on his clothes—even four years later. As I was holding onto Reuben's tiny baby grow, I sensed Jesus was trying to tell me that our heartache is like a sweet aroma when it is brought to him.

This brings me back to the Bible story of the woman weeping and washing Jesus' feet with her tears. She went on to pour out expensive perfume on Jesus' feet. The aroma must have been intensely beautiful. It wasn't just perfume she was pouring out—it was her shame and lack of self-worth. She was crying for mercy. For so long, she had been shamed by her community. And so, pouring out all her brokenness and shame upon the feet of Jesus was a prayer for restoration. Our fragments have an aroma. When we bring them to Jesus, it is, to him, sweet.

The fact of our broken hearts is a reason to worship Jesus, and to pour out our brokenness upon him. One of the disciples said that pouring an expensive perfume out was a waste. Others may say that crying and pouring out your brokenness to God is a waste, or that being vulnerable with others is a shameful thing to do. But none of this is a waste, because God wants to care for your broken heart.

In-between grief and hope, nothing is wasted. In fact, things are put back together. As we pour out our brokenness, our hearts become worshipful. What others see as waste rises up to Jesus as the aroma of worship.

References:

[15] John 6:12 (NIV): 'When they had all had enough to eat, he said to his disciples, "Gather the pieces that are left over. Let nothing be wasted."'

CHAPTER 8

Facing Grief

If you don't face your grief, it will find a way to face you. Coming face to face with grief is a key part of accepting loss. But facing grief comes with the fear of losing your loved one for good.

I was having another vivid dream. I was on a boat, and I was in the middle of a war. From every point, I was being chased down by enemies who were trying to kill me, all while I was facing my worst fear: the sea. I am terrified of swimming in the ocean, but it was my only way out. I had a decision to make: I could either get off the boat and swim for freedom, or stay on the boat and die. I made the decision to get off the boat and go into the shallow water; to face my fear. As I anxiously turned my head around to make sure I was safe, I saw, to my surprise, that I wasn't alone. The most beautiful angel was with me and I was overcome with both awe and fear. I wanted to turn away, but my spirit felt safe. As I looked at the angel's pure white hair and into their crystal blue eyes, I knew that this was a holy moment. I felt protected and at peace. Suddenly, with a steady and authoritative voice, he said, 'I have two swords'. Without hesitation, the angel thrust them straight into the enemy standing behind me. I was safe, and I wasn't alone! I was aware that I was carrying Reuben in my hands under the water. I drew him out of the water, and at that moment, realised he had died. Then I woke up.

This was a healing moment for me. It helped me realise that I was holding onto grief tightly. I hadn't found it easy to face what had happened. Even though I had been learning how to cry and how to grieve with God, I hadn't found the courage to surrender the pain I was holding on to. It was like I had a knife in my stomach, which I was able to cry about to God—to tell him of the pain—without letting Him take it out and heal the wound.

Getting out of the boat in my dream represented surrender. That's why I felt confronted by fear at the thought of stepping out; the fear of more suffering and of experiencing more loneliness. I was at my lowest emotionally when I had this dream, and I felt extremely vulnerable. There is a story in the Bible in which we are told about a time when the disciples were afraid. They were on a boat during a stormy night, and they became fearful when they saw Jesus walk towards them on the water. I can imagine that in their panic they wondered what was coming towards them until they recognised Jesus' voice. Sometimes fear can affect our vision; it can make us see what isn't there. The disciples thought that they were seeing a ghost until Jesus said, 'Don't be afraid. Take courage. I am here!' [16]. Jesus speaks the same words over you and your fear. He encourages you to go towards him. The fear that holds you back from knowing Jesus is exactly what God wants you to face. Peter, Jesus' disciple, was feeling extra confident and considered walking towards Jesus on the water. Courageously, Peter faced his fear and stepped out onto the water. He was afraid, but he had the courage to walk toward Jesus in his fear. God is calling us to walk towards him despite the fears that are holding us down—even if the thought of sinking into the pain of loss feels scary. However, you won't be endlessly walking into wave after wave. Instead, you will be walking towards Him. Walking towards God on the water may look like trusting God with the person you have lost. Trust that they are safe in heaven. Right now, you deserve the space to heal fully. Jesus is in the centre of all our suffering, and he is the reason to hope again. We read in Matthew 14 that Jesus immediately grabbed Peter's hand after he succumbed to fear and began to sink into the waters. Jesus, with intention, will grab your hand to pull you to the safety of his love.

King David, in the Psalms, writes prayers of lament in his moments of hopelessness and despair. On one occasion, he was being hunted down by a jealous King. He called for God to take action, saying, 'God, take up your shield and buckler, and rise for my help! Draw the spear and javelin against my pursuers! Say to my soul, "I am your salvation!"' (Psalm 35:2-3). I believe that whatever is hunting you down and stopping you from grieving—whether that be fear, anxiety, or depression—can be overcome. You don't have to face it alone. God will help you face your grief in a beautiful way. Sometimes we cling to our grief as if it is our saviour, but it is only God that saves us.

A time to surrender

Grief can weigh you down. I was holding on to mine as I tried to swim through the water in my dream. I didn't realise until I drew Reuben out of the water. At that moment, I understood that to fully surrender, I had to lay down what was weighing me down.

Surrender, for me, meant giving Reuben to Jesus. And so I did this through prayer. I told God that I was ready to hand over Reuben to Him. It wasn't a huge moment on the surface. But, spiritually, I knew I had made room for God to bring healing.

When we surrender our deepest wounds to God, there is an abundance of healing that takes place in our lives. When Moses was a baby, Pharaoh tried to kill all first-born Israelite boys. Moses survived this ordeal. Moses' mother had to let Moses go to prevent him from eventually being caught and killed. She placed Moses in a basket upon a river while his sister watched her brother float away. Where the water led Moses is a miracle. Pharaoh's daughter found Moses and 'drew him out of the water' [17]. She had compassion for Moses and wanted to take care of him, but she needed someone to nurse the baby. Moses' sister, who had followed the basket, was able to request that his mother take care of him.

I can imagine the happiness that filled Moses' mother when she would have realised that she would get to be with her son for a little while longer. Sadly, the day would still come when she would have to give him back to Pharaoh's household to be raised as an Egyptian.

Because God was with him, Moses ended up right where he needed to be. When his mother surrendered, God took the opportunity to make a way for Moses to be with his mum while being in the position to become an Egyptian who would lead his people out of Egypt and into the Promised Land. When we choose to surrender our grief, we allow God to take it away. That will always be better than holding it close. If Moses' mother had decided to hold Moses close, he could have been killed, and he wouldn't be able to bring freedom to the Israelites. I found that when I had the courage to start the process of letting go, I gradually became more able to listen to others who had grieved. That enabled me to write this book. I realised that for most of my life, I hadn't given loss a thought; it was never on my agenda to consider grief. When I trusted God with my wounds, He started trusting me with those who were grieving deeply. People would ask me about how many children I had, and I would bravely say that I had three but that Reuben was sadly in heaven. In many of these conversations, people would open up about how they also had lost a baby, and with every conversation came more healing. Grief naturally started to come into my conversations, not in a heavy way, but in a beautiful way.

Freely speaking about our stories of pain and loss gives less power to our struggle and more power to the hope that we are given from above. Your own story in learning to grieve will always give you the opportunity to help others heal.

References:

[16] Matthew 14:27 (NLT): 'But Jesus spoke to them at once. "Don't be afraid," he said. "Take courage. I am here!"'

[17] Exodus 2:5 (NIV): 'Then Pharaoh's daughter went down to the Nile to bathe, and her attendants were walking along the riverbank. She saw the basket among the reeds and sent her female slave to get it.'

CHAPTER 9

Saying Goodbye

I am not a huge fan of goodbyes. I am an emotional weeping mess when it comes to the simplest of them. For the past few years, we have been taking my mum on holiday with us. After a long week of being together, I always cry when she leaves to go home. Almost every time I leave her, I say, 'I will see you in a few weeks, and I will ring you tomorrow'. The promise that I would see her again and the fact that I'd hear her voice the next day made the goodbyes easier and lighter. In some sense, I never really said goodbyes. My goodbyes sounded more like, 'See you soon'. The same is true when the time came to say goodbye to Reuben. I didn't know how to say goodbye, so I didn't say it with words. The day Reuben died, I understood that I would never hold him again, but in my heart, I couldn't find it in me to say my final goodbyes. I was in denial. I wanted my goodbye to Reuben to be as special as the day he came into this world. But no moment was special enough. So I held the memory of him close. Regularly, I would hold his tiny baby grows close to my chest, close my eyes, and pretend he was there. I was terrified that if I said the words goodbye, I wouldn't feel as close to him. I wanted to be ready, and I wanted it to feel right! The thought of actually 'letting go' made me feel I had no control. Mentally, I would freeze, and then I would put saying goodbye off a little longer.

Goodbyes are so difficult. For me, saying goodbye meant acknowledging the truth that Reuben was gone. When we acknowledge the truth about something painful, it becomes more real, and that means having to face it. For a long time, I just didn't know how to do all this. It seemed so final, and I was so scared I wouldn't do justice to Reuben's loss. I am reminded of a moment in the Bible when Herod ordered that all boys under the age of two were to be killed. The writer of the story mentions a prophecy from Jeremiah in which a grieving mother, Rachel, was heard weeping for her children. It says that she refused to be comforted. I understand that. It's a very human response to certain things. Comfort is sometimes needed, but most of the time, weeping without consolation for pain is a part of the healing journey. It sometimes feels like it's the only thing we have left after someone we love dies. It's okay not to want to be okay. There's grace for the journey which God will provide.

About four years after Reuben died, I went to a church conference with a heavy heart. I had been going through a hard patch whilst writing this book and had been revisiting each moment of my grief. I was reminded that, in my dream, I had realised that I had kept hold of Reuben after I lifted him out of the water. Jesus was reminding me to let go of the pain I had held for so long, but I was angry and was struggling with the idea. In the same vision, I imagined Jesus in a robe with Reuben in the arms of Jesus. Reuben was full of joy. The word that comes to my mind is 'Celebration'. As Reuben was looking at me, a sense of the celebratory was bursting through his eyes, and I could feel the strength within him. I knew deep down that it was time to say goodbye and let go of some of the pain that I had been carrying. 'Goodbye' is precisely the word I needed the courage to say, but it had power over me. I had attached it to fear of deeper loss, and I wasn't sure if I wanted this change. However, I found the courage to say goodbye to Reuben, with God's help. Whether my mind had made this moment in my vision by itself, or whether God had prepared it for me, I am grateful that I got to say my goodbyes. The next day felt like the day after I buried Reuben. I was exhausted.

I found that there is grace around the timing of our goodbyes. There's no exact time when we should say goodbye and there's no right way to say goodbye. God allows us to hold on to the pain if we want to, and He is there when we are ready so that we do not have to say goodbye alone. Saying goodbye doesn't mean that we will never feel pain again, but when we involve God, we don't have to carry the pain alone.

Maybe you have said your goodbyes, or, like me, maybe you have lived in denial for a long period and have become fearful of saying goodbye. I encourage you to use this space to invite Jesus into your fear of saying goodbye. Tell Jesus what you need and how you would like to say goodbye. I like imagery—using the visual is the way I work. But you may find it helpful to write a letter, light a candle, or to simply hold a picture of the person you have lost while taking a moment to say goodbye.

I have now found that I have space to heal because I am not carrying the full weight of my loss. I have more room for God's love in my life, and that has been a marvellously beautiful part of my journey. Each day I am reminded that He is walking with me, that I don't have to walk alone. Since the day I said goodbye, I have felt a sense of newness, a sense of new mercy, and a new beginning that is both freeing and exciting.

I think of how Jesus said his goodbyes to his disciples. He did it without ever really leaving. He left His Holy Spirit so that we could continue to know him while he was gone; we carry him in our hearts. Our loved ones that leave us leave a part of themselves with us. When we say goodbye, we say goodbye to the physical, the emotional, and so much more. We say goodbye to the body we once held when they were sick and the face we wiped tears from when they were sad. We say goodbye to years of life, to memories of holidays and the holidays that were never taken. We say goodbye to unbaked birthday cakes and to the first days of school. We say goodbye to everything that could have been. But we hold on to the memories created, the clothes once worn and the pictures that hang on our wall that remind us of who they once were.

Saying goodbye is brave, and it may mean saying a lifetime of goodbyes. But God has enough grace and love for us on that journey of grief.

SECTION 3

LONGING FOR HOPE

CHAPTER 10

In-Between Spaces

There's a place in-between all our sorrow and all our grief where we grow thirsty for hope. Some say time is a healer, but I have found that time makes the longing to be with loved ones stronger. In the early days of loss, you remember the touch and smell of your loved one. But the memories become less clear as time passes. The space between you and your loved one becomes greater, and the longing for them grows more intense.

The longing to be with Reuben used to strike me daily. Seeing my children laugh and thrive would make me long to see Reuben running around joyfully with them. The hardest moments were when I put my children to bed. Storytime is the most fun part of the day, and I love making up funny characters and using the stories to encourage my children about their strengths. Even now, four years on, it still feels like someone is missing during those moments. I catch my mind running wild as I imagine Reuben and me creating memories together. We build sandcastles together during our summer holidays, then go and get an ice cream. I wonder what flavour he would choose. I wonder what life would be like with him here. Sometimes, during the most mundane moments of the day, you remember that the person you've lost was born and had a purpose in this life; that you got to be a part of it—even if it was just for a short while. The beautiful truth is that our loved ones are always with us, whether in memory or in imagination.

It was an ordinary day. I had done the washing and the cleaning before doing crafts with my youngest. I was waiting for my eldest, Elijah, to return from school, and on this particular day, he brought me home a handmade card. On the front of the card was a drawing of himself in our family house with Jesus beside him. Just above the house he drew Reuben into heaven, and Jesus was beside him too. On the next page, Elijah and Bella (my youngest) were drawn inside a rocket, and they were going to visit Reuben in heaven, which, in the drawing, was represented by a door in the sky with the stars surrounding it. As a child, Elijah understood that we are separated from heaven and that it is a different place, but he also understood that Jesus is here with us on earth as well as in heaven with Reuben. This is such a beautiful truth that we need to grab hold of. This reminded me that there is an opportunity to get closer to Jesus in the in-between.

The 'in-between place' in life is hard to navigate; coming to terms with the distance between ourselves and the people we have lost is hard to navigate. Paul, a man who preached the gospel even in his suffering, speaks about this same thing from a different point of view when he talks about longing to be with Jesus. In Philippians 1, he says, 'I am hard pressed between the two. My desire is to depart and be with Christ, for that is far better. But to remain in the flesh is more necessary on your account' [18]. He goes on to explain the benefits of being in heaven and the benefits of being here on earth. The longing for both is completely normal, and I know I have more than once experienced the desire to be in both places.

Like my son, Elijah, beautifully reminded us, there is an opportunity to become closer to Jesus in the in-between. Jesus is the one that stands between you and your loved ones. He's the only one who can satisfy the longing within, and he will satisfy that longing. We are told in

James 4:8 that when we draw close to God, God will draw close to us. When Jesus went to heaven, he left his Holy Spirit as a gift so we could have access to the fullness of God. So, when we long for more hope, the Holy Spirit comes close to us. When we think about the things that we want but can't have, it creates a frustrating hunger that cannot be satisfied. But when we draw close to God, we are filled with His spirit, which brings a peace that surpasses all of our understanding. In Philippians 4:7, we are told that the peace that comes through knowing God will also guard our hearts and minds. Our hearts and minds are fragile when we are grieving and longing for hope, so we need the peace that surpasses our heartbreak and unanswered questions. I encourage you to use this moment to invite Jesus and his spirit to bring the peace he offers to you.

Desperation in the In-Between

There was once a woman desperate for God to hear her voice. Her name was Hagar, and she was a slave to a man named Abraham. God had promised Abraham children, and his wife Sarah was longing for the promise to come to fruition. However, Sarah had grown impatient after many years of waiting. She told her husband to have a baby with her servant Hagar so that she no longer had to wait. After Hagar gave birth, Sarah herself became pregnant, and she eventually got what she was hoping for: a son named Isaac. She was happy for a while, but then her jealousy grew more fierce by the day because she did not want her son to share his inheritance with Hagar's son. This meant Hagar was thrown out with her child, and eventually, Hagar ran out of water and food. Hagar's child was dying of thirst, and in her desperation and grief, she placed her son under a tree while she sat under another to pray, since she couldn't bear the sight of her son dying. Scripture says that God heard the boy's cries, and the angel of

God said to Hagar, 'Fear not, for God has heard your boy's voice from where he is' (Genesis 21:17).

When Hagar put space between her and her son's condition, as hard as it was, God spoke into her situation. It also tells us in Genesis 21:19 that God opened her eyes to see a well with which she could fill her bottle and give her son a drink. Both her thirst and her longing to be heard were quenched.

When Reuben was first born, he was seriously sick and couldn't breathe alone. The fact of the space between my bed and Reuben's life-saving machines was intensely painful. Reuben would cry out, but his cries were silent because of his condition. Everything within me wanted to hold him and comfort him, but I was unable to. I knew he wanted to be held, and I couldn't give him that. All I could do was pray that he would know the Father's love as he lay there. All the while, I would sing to him so he knew I was close.

Sometimes, however, space is what we need to think and see clearly. Hagar, in distancing herself from her son, made space to hear God's voice and direction in her life. Often, when it comes to longing to see God move, making space is the last thing we want to think about. In my own healing journey, I initially wanted to keep myself distracted. Space was something that scared me because it meant processing my thoughts and feelings. The angel told Hagar that her son's prayers had been answered. He didn't say that her prayers were answered. I'm not sure why he said this, but I think the lesson here is the reminder that our loved ones have their own voices alongside ours. When we are in agony, we tend only to hear our own groans and despair. This scripture helps us realise that we are not suffering alone. This encouraged me because it reminded me that Reuben had his own voice and his own response to God. We know from Luke 1:41 that when Elizabeth heard

Mary's voice, the baby in her womb (John) responded to the Holy Spirit and leapt. It's hard for us to understand how this could happen, and I have many questions about it. But there is one thing we can be sure of, and that is that God hears our prayers and the prayers of our children, no matter how old they may be. In Psalm 107:9, we read that God 'satisfies the longing soul, and the hungry soul he fills with good things.' The Hebrew used for 'longing' here is a form of 'shakak', which means 'to thirst'. Hagar thirsted for water, and this paints a picture of spiritual thirst. When we are grieving, we are thirsty, and we don't always have the strength to drink. But God will draw close to us and show us the well from which we can drink. Hagar had lost her favour and her home, and she very nearly lost her son. But she had hope in God. Why? Because of God's faithfulness. My child didn't get healed on this side of heaven, but I know for sure that he is healed in heaven. God is still faithful. Not because of what He's done, but because of who He is. He has chosen to be our Father, our friend, and our comforter. Even in all the suffering, He chooses to listen and be faithful to His children.

The reason that we can struggle with God's faithfulness (trust me, I have), is that we measure God's faithfulness against our expectations of who He should be and what He should do for us. I used to say, 'God loves me, so I know my child will live.' But this isn't true! Bad things can happen daily to God's people. But He still loves us. God's love isn't a shield from pain and suffering. It was never meant to be. God's love is meant for our salvation. His love can pierce the darkness and bring light to the suffering we endure. It's always consistent, and never-changing.

We are all 'in-between'. We are all hoping that one day we'll see our loved ones on the other side, and that longing can be incredibly painful. God's faithfulness may not look like a healed loved one, but His faithfulness stands in the space you find yourself in. His faithfulness exists because God exists. I encourage you to speak of His faithfulness in praise. I am not saying that you should write a list of all the physical things we have received through or alongside His faithfulness because things can be taken away, and His faithfulness isn't measured by the things that we have. Bless Him in the emptiness, the suffering, and the heartache. Praise God because He chose you, and because He's your Father.

References:

[18] Philippians 1:23-24 (ESV): 'I am hard pressed between the two. My desire is to depart and be with Christ, for that is far better. But to remain in the flesh is more necessary on your account.'

CHAPTER 11

Present Hope

Sometimes, in the middle of all the grief, it can feel like hope has been put on hold. It's like when a wedding has to be postponed until further notice, and so all wedding planning stops. It's not God's desire to withhold hope, but sadly, this can feel like the reality for many of us. As a result, we can fall into the trap of putting our hope in our plans for the future rather than in God. Planning for the future can feel so life-giving, and rightly so. There is a place for it. However, this rabbit hole can lead to never stepping into the present, and it can distract us from the hope that God wants to give.

The future is withheld from us because only God knows what is before us. We cannot be in tomorrow just because we want to be. Tomorrow is hidden from us until it comes. I could conclude this chapter with a verse about trusting in God, but, as we know, things aren't that simple. Trust is not all that easy when you have been disappointed.

Our failure to have hope is often linked with our lack of trust in God. If our hopes are tied to our wants and needs, then suffering and disappointment will cause us to lose our hope when they become heavy burdens. When hope is grounded in a trust-filled relationship with Jesus, it will not move. In Hebrews 10:23 (NIV), we read, 'Let us hold unswervingly to the hope we profess, for he who promised is faithful'. This hope is our salvation and our inheritance. If we put our trust in the God that made us children of God, then surely our hope is alive.

Dealing with Disappointment

Going through disappointment wasn't something new to me, and everyone has experienced disappointment throughout their lives. However, I had never really experienced disappointment with God until Reuben passed away. I hoped and longed for Reuben to have a long and love-filled life here with us, but what I was left with was a shattering disappointment.

It was like the support and security of my body and soul had been taken away. When a wall is knocked down in a house, and it isn't shored up, the whole structure of the house is unsound. I felt it was something like this house. God had been where I had put my trust for so long, and as soon as I lost Reuben, that trust went. I didn't realise it at the time, but I also started to fear death during every waking moment. I was terrified that I wouldn't have any more children. I would sit up at night watching Elijah breathe. Once, I became convinced that he had died in his sleep. I thought I was losing my mind. My security had gone, and I had put my trust in myself instead of in God.

* * *

I want to look at a story about two sisters who longed for Jesus to come to them but were disappointed. What interests me is Jesus' response to those sisters. Jesus had a close friendship with a guy called Lazarus, who had become sick. Lazarus' sisters—Mary and Martha—sent a messenger to Jesus, saying, 'Lord, the one you love is sick' [19]. Jesus decided to stay where he was for a few more days, and by the time he had made his way to Lazarus, it was too late. Lazarus had died. Martha said to Jesus, 'Lord...if you had been here, my brother would not have died' (v. 21). This statement is something we can relate to. How can God allow death? Surely, if God were here with us, our loved ones wouldn't have died in the first place. In response to the sisters, Jesus said these stunning words: 'I am the resurrection and the life. He who believes in me will live, even though he dies, and whoever lives and believes in me will never die' [20].

When our trust is in God alone, we remain in the promise that whoever believes and trusts in Him will live. Even in death, we will live. In Romans 15:13 (NLT), we read that the source of hope (God) will fill us with joy and peace as we trust in him. It also says that we will overflow with confident hope through the power of the Holy Spirit.

When we choose to trust in God over taking control, we receive a confident hope; a sure hope that goes beyond the limits of our emotions and circumstances and gives us the faith to know the source of all hope.

God at Work

I had a slight bleed when I was just halfway through my pregnancy. Because the pregnancy was high-risk, I went to the hospital. I was there for hours before I was seen. When you're under 20 weeks, you can't yet visit the maternity ward, and so I had to wait in general A&E while more urgent cases were dealt with. I was so worried that I was miscarrying. It was such a traumatic experience. I saw a pregnant girl come through the side door who was seen instantly. In a fit of rage, I walked out of A&E in tears. I couldn't understand why my baby was less critical than hers. I knew that they thought that my baby had no chance of living and were consequently pushing me down the priority list.

While I was sitting on a broken old bench, a lady came over to see if I was okay. I explained my situation, and then she said that it was her daughter that had just been rushed in. Her daughter had a very high-risk pregnancy and was told she would never be pregnant. Her baby was in danger. I felt so terrible and selfish that I stormed out of the hospital, and I sheepishly went back in to wait my turn. After a couple more hours, I was eventually seen. As I was being treated, I saw the girl in a cubicle. I sensed that I should pray for her baby, so I went over and asked if I could pray for protection for her unborn child. She said yes. Our babies were due at around the same time, but her child lived, and mine didn't. I had prayed to the same God for the health and life of them both, but each prayer saw a different outcome.

When we live in confident hope, we can reach out beyond our limitations to bring hope into other people's lives. I can't say that it was my prayer specifically that changed the course of this other baby's future, but I am confident God did change their future. We can be in restricted places, longing for our own healing and still reach out to God in confident hope. Your restrictions do not need to determine your path. Placing your hope in God will guide your way and impact those around you.

God promises in Jeremiah 29:11 that God wants to give us a future with hope. This verse was spoken to a people going through a season of limitation. These people lived in exile and had been given false encouragement explaining that they would soon leave exile. A man of God named Jeremiah, however, came to them to provide them with real encouragement. Unfortunately, he told them that they had to stay in exile for a while longer, but that this didn't mean that they couldn't have hope. The same truth applies to us. God gives us hope in the middle of our suffering. The people in exile could make plans for their lives, but only within the limitations of exile. Our first response to restriction and limitation is to try and break out of it and gain our freedom. However, what if there is freedom to be found within this restriction?

As I write this, most of us have just spent more than two years with restrictions all around us as we have lived the nightmare of COVID.

Under these, the world had to adapt to a new way of living. Many people have started to see that family and community are the most important things. We clung to our loved ones as we began to realise how easily they could be taken from us. We no longer took for granted the opportunities we had to spend time with one another.

During this time, I asked myself a question which I want to ask you: what opportunities do your current restrictions give you to reach out to others with hope? Can you reach out to someone who is in your shoes? Or maybe you can reach out to someone closer to home?

The restrictions and fear I experienced during my trials told me I was alone. But confident hope told me that there was a loving family and community surrounding me. Holding back hope can lead to fear, and fear lies. The lies want us to believe we are not deserving of hope, but we are!

References:

[19] John 11:3 (NIV): 'So the sisters sent word to Jesus, "Lord, the one you love is sick."'

[20] John 11:25 (NIV): 'Jesus said to her, "I am the resurrection and the life. The one who believes in me will live, even though they die."'

CHAPTER 12

Anchored Hope

The hope you long for can become a reality. The author of Hebrews tells us that 'hope is an anchor' and that it 'makes us firm and secure' (Hebrews 6:19). That verse really spoke to me one day. As I was meditating on it, I felt Jesus say to me that prayer activates hope.

An anchored boat won't be moved, even when a storm comes. If Jesus is our hope, then he is also our anchor. If Jesus is our anchor, it is he who stops us from being tossed about by the storm of grief. An anchor that stays in the boat during a storm serves no purpose—it was made to be used. When we pray in the middle of a storm, it's like we activate the anchor and allow it to steady our ship. Jesus can hold us steadfast so that we aren't blown around and so that we aren't at the mercy of the storm.

Beyond this, he carries the weight of our grief. In my own grief, I tried to take the weight of death upon myself. After Reuben's death, I suffered from severe fatigue. Some days I couldn't lift my body out of bed without being in pain, and other days I walked around half awake. I tried to find joy some days but, by lunchtime, I would find myself weary and fatigued again. Jesus said the following words to me, and I believe he wants to say them to you too: 'Come to me, all you who are weary and burdened, and I will give you rest. Take my yoke upon you and learn from me, for I am gentle and humble in heart, and you will find rest for your souls. For my yoke is easy, and my burden is light' (Matthew 11:28-30 NIV). Jesus bears the weight of our sin, brokenness, and suffering so that we don't have to.

Prayer can also transport us into the inner sanctuary of God. When I meet the undercurrents of grief, I find that prayer reorientates me and my body; a body that wanted to give up on itself. Prayer gave my mind respite from the torment, and my heart was lifted into the sweet presence of Jesus. Communication with Jesus saved my life, and the place of prayer became a safe haven for my shattered heart.

However, that didn't mean all my prayers were answered, and I don't have a pithy quote that can explain why many of our prayers don't get answered. I can't pretend to understand or explain, and if I am honest, I don't think I want to know. I believe the answers that are hidden from us are the mysteries that compel us to draw close to the Father's heart. Not knowing forces us to be weak, and, as a result, we have no choice but to put our strength in God alone. When, in prayer, we rest in the knowledge of who God says He is—even when we do not always see our prayers answered—we experience the safety of prayer.

The key is to keep praying despite our circumstances and to choose to trust God and every promise he stands for. A question I once asked myself is: Am I trusting that I will receive answers to my prayers, or am I trusting that God will be who He promises to be? The truth is that our trust can be misplaced, and this can lead to our sense of trust becoming warped. We can allow our experience of unanswered prayer to disfigure our sense of trust, or we can trust despite unanswered prayer. Our trust is not based on being caught when we fall. Our trust is based on the promise that Jesus will fall with us and then give us the strength to get back on our feet. So, even in our darkest moments, we can choose to pray and to have hope in our God.

A prayer conceived in hope would look much like a prayer spoken in Luke 22: 'Father, if you are willing, please take this cup of suffering away from me. Yet I want your will to be done, not mine' [21].

Jesus longed for his suffering to end, but somehow, within the pain, he chose to pray: 'Your will, not mine.' Out of that prayer came the hope of salvation that we cling to. We also have a choice to pray such prayers from our place of suffering, even if they are as simple and as short as the words Jesus chose to pray.

The morning after Reuben had passed, we had a choice: stay longer with him, or leave. We'd spent the night holding his tiny still body, and it was too hard and too painful to stay any longer. I prayed silently, and then a thought landed in my head. It was a Sunday morning, and I thought we should go to the nearest church. So that's what we did. We arrived at the church and sat down on our chairs. An older man and woman came to sit with us. They introduced themselves as Carole and Barry, and we told them about Reuben and that we'd come straight from the hospital. They explained that they had lost a baby girl when they were younger. They stayed and worshipped, and they held our hands throughout the service. During his talk, the pastor explained that his dad had died a few years ago, and he spoke about his journey of loss to encourage the congregation to stick with faith—even in painful times. We have been friends with Carole and Barry ever since, and I will be forever grateful that I prayed that prayer that morning and decided to go to that church.

God didn't answer my prayers of healing for Reuben, but he did send friends, comfort, and kindness that morning. Since Reuben has passed, prayer is something I still cling to. Prayer hasn't lost its power just because my prayers weren't answered. I still struggle to understand why Reuben had to die; to understand the nature of injustice, sickness, and of death. But regardless, I know that prayer is a lifeline for me.

I like to see prayer as a conversation with a friend. When we speak with the people we love, we don't demand a gift at the end of the chat. More often, we may come away inspired or empowered. Sometimes the conversation is just about listening or focusing our attention on the other person. Often we leave with words of theirs to ponder on. Jesus is our friend, and he wants to be a part of our lives and to be having conversations with us along the way. That morning after Reuben had died, I believe I was having a conversation with a Father and my friend who, at that time, wanted me to know His love and comfort. He couldn't physically come and sit in the hospital with me, but he sent me Carole, Barry, and the pastor, all of whom spoke words of comfort and kindness to me, which left me feeling hopeful.

It's Hard to Pray

All of this isn't to say that there haven't been moments of my grief in which I haven't wanted to pray. The shock of grief can sometimes silence you. For a time I felt I couldn't trust God with my prayers, so I was silent until I was ready. And that's okay! There's no shame in not feeling like talking. My husband and I are quite comfortable spending time together without talking—we know we love each other without having to always share words.

We don't always have to raise our voices and our hands to God in order to be heard. Romans 8:26 says that even when we don't know what to pray, God hears our wordless groans. When God is a part of you, He's always a part of you, and He will not disappear in our suffering.

I have often said that I can feel held and comforted by Jesus while still feeling utterly broken. As a result, my prayer life hasn't always been lively. Sometimes, my prayers are spoken as if my face was pressed up against a window. They are the grumblings of someone who is fed up with life and yet is trying hard to hang in there. I remember sometimes starting a conversation with God and ending it in the same sentence—I was just too tired to carry on.

Prayer can look vibrant, and it can look grey. Jesus doesn't really have a preference. He is listening anyway. Prayer is there for you to connect and feel secure even in the depths of grief. God is the anchor in your situation, and that anchor is activated through prayer. You don't need a huge amount of faith—Jesus said that faith that is as small as a mustard seed can move mountains (Matthew 17:20).

Hope provided me with small moments of joy, helped me take time to play with my children, and gave me the energy to eat a full meal. Those moments fuelled by hope were soon adjoined to become my everyday. Now I look back and see how prayer has been a medicine for my sick heart and mind. I encourage you to hang in there and to reach out in prayer, even if it involves nothing more than a half-awake or angry grumble, and even if there are no words. Position your heart towards Jesus, and he will hear the words behind the silence.

References:

[21] Luke 22:42 (NLT): 'Father, if you are willing, please take this cup of suffering away from me. Yet I want your will to be done, not mine.'

SECTION FOUR

LEANING INTO JESUS

CHAPTER 13

Rise and Walk

It may seem that being asked to 'rise and walk' is contradictory to leaning on Jesus. But what I would like to suggest is that when we do it with God's help, rising and walking out of despair is the same as leaning on Jesus; on God. When we rise and walk with God, we do so whilst leaning on the one that gives us the ability to live within grief. The word 'rising' can refer to being elevated. Isaiah speaks of rising in this way: 'But those who keep waiting for the Lord will renew their strength. Then they'll soar on wings like eagles; they'll run and not grow weary; they'll walk and not grow tired.'[22] This is the image I want you to have in your mind when you read this chapter. God's will for us is to rise and walk with confidence onto his wings whilst we are in our grief.

There will be a time when we must be willing to 'rise and walk' out of our grief, but this doesn't mean that we have to do so in our own strength. We have the option to lean upon Jesus; to rest on his wings of grace. I have had two c-sections, and the pain of trying to walk after surgery is unbearable. Well, it feels impossible at the least. I remember the pain so vividly that the thought still makes me nauseous. I was told that walking after surgery would improve the healing process and that I would become stronger if I practised walking in small amounts each day. I can confirm this is true. But this doesn't change the fact that the burning sensations and stabbing pains are agonising during those first steps. The same pain travelled through my entire body when I had to rise from the side of my son's grave. I felt crippled by the knowledge that I would never see him again. After choosing to 'rise,' I did not fear re-entering grief again. I wasn't afraid of knowing grief. I just wanted to step into more than a life of agony. Re-entering grief is always a possibility, but it is important to have the courage to keep rising when you have been swept into a sadness that seems impossible to leave. I am talking about taking those brave steps towards facing pain and those brave steps out of a place of sorrow towards re-entering normal everyday life.

I need you to know that there is no shame in being stuck in your pain. In fact, grief is a process we need to respect. I had many days in which my pain felt like sinking sand and in which I crawled out of bed feeling disoriented. I had to drag myself to the bathroom and force my feet to move down our narrow staircase into the kitchen to prepare breakfast for my family. Each movement was a brave one in my eyes: one step brought me closer to productivity, while the other brought me closer to healing. Each step represented a choice to keep going even though my body wanted to stay still and numb the pain. Each step reminded me of the suffering I felt because it was so hard to keep going, but each step also reminded me of the love that existed in the midst of my sorrow.

I would sometimes be transported back to a place of pain and deep grief unexpectedly. I'd be walking down the street, see a family of three, and then feel an overwhelming sadness. I soon realised that I had to make a choice to 'rise' after I gave myself time to digest my loss again. That meant giving myself permission to acknowledge the pain and then giving myself permission to re-enter my present life.

Those moments of pain meant Reuben still existed in my world and in daily life. I gave my memories—my pain—a place to rest within me. A home, you could say. There is a safe in which it lies. It's the place where

I hold the pain and suffering, but it's also the place in which I hold a huge amount of gratitude for Reuben's life.

In Acts, we are told a story about a man who did not have the ability to walk [23]. While he was physically crippled, he was probably also emotionally crippled due to the way society would likely have treated him. He would sit and wait at the same gate every day for someone to provide for his needs. One day, Peter and John (Jesus' disciples and friends) happened to be in the area on their way to the temple. As they passed him, he asked them for money. The scripture tells us: 'Peter directed his gaze at him, as did John, and said, "Look at us." And he fixed his attention on them, expecting to receive something from them. But Peter said, "I have no silver and gold, but what I do have I give to you. In the name of Jesus Christ of Nazareth, rise up and walk!"'

Let's pause for a moment and remember the times we enter into sadness, which is like sinking sand and how hard it is to carry on at times. The pain can paralyse you. I found I would get stuck in what I call a mad maze of the mind in which I relived traumatic moments. Everything around me would carry on as normal, and I would be alone in my memories. Recently, we have heard the devastating news that my mum has terminal lung cancer. The doctors think she has very little time left to live. There are moments when I see an elderly woman with her daughter, for example, and I am stung by grief as I think about the fact that my mum and I will never experience what they are experiencing. 'Rising' isn't easy when your body is frozen with pain. Daily I find myself sitting like the paralysed beggar at my own gate waiting for some kind of miracle to happen—hoping to be given better news and to be living a brighter day. I know I'm not the only one in a state of grief who finds that they are a little desperate for something more.

Looking at the scripture in Acts 3, we see four poignant moments: the man is carried (1), then he looks (2), and he rises (3) before finally walking (4). Each moment is equally important and can teach us something.

Being Carried

The man at the gate was waiting for something, but he was never going to get what he was waiting for with his own ability. We are told that this man was lame from birth and that he was carried to the beautiful gate daily so he could beg. He had to rely on someone to carry him, and without that, he wouldn't have had the opportunity to look, rise, and walk.

God can give our community the strength and love to carry us to a place of healing. But, if we are honest, it's not always the case that this happens. Especially when our sorrows isolate us from those we love. No matter what, however, God will carry us. In Isaiah 40, we read, 'He will tend his flock like a shepherd; he will gather the lambs in his arms; he will carry them in his bosom, and gently lead those that are with young.' [24]. We know that Jesus is the shepherd who has come to give us 'life...to the full' (John 10)[25]. Just as a young child must constantly learn how to handle their emotions, we too must continually learn. I soon realised that I had to learn to be kind to myself. I was young in my grief. I had never lost a child before, and my body, mind, and spirit needed to be gently led. Jesus is the gentle guide, carrying us in his arms and allowing us time and grace to heal. A comfort I took from the words of Isaiah is the way it describes being carried in God's 'bosom' in the manner a mother would carry a child close to her chest; a way of being carried which allows the child to be comforted by the mother's heartbeat. If we allow ourselves to trust God to carry us, we will be safe in His arms.

Look

We read in Acts 3:5 that the crippled man looked at Peter and John expecting something from them. Presumably, he expected money—something which would help with the basics of survival, like food and shelter. However, they didn't have what the man wanted. Peter and John didn't give him 'silver and gold', but something far more precious: healing for his body. A question I ask myself often is this: On what is my gaze fixed? Am I gazing at the pain that paralyses me, or am I choosing to look to Jesus as an act of faith while trusting that he can provide for both my daily needs and something much bigger?

When Reuben died, I felt the loneliest I had ever felt. For a long time, I put pressure on myself to replace the old friends my grief had distanced me from, and I started looking for a perfect friend. Instead, Jesus himself showed me what a good friend was through my friendship with him. In my desperation, I had pushed friends away, and what Jesus wanted me to do was look at him. Peter and John weren't themselves the answer to this man's problem. They were a part of the solution, but ultimately, it was Jesus who made him 'rise and walk'.

Rise

One of the reasons why it is so hard to 'rise' in the midst of suffering is that the sadness is beyond our understanding. In my experience, the unknown had a tendency to make me feel weak. We need supernatural strength to rise. When Jesus chose to die for our sins, he also rose from the dead for our suffering so that we could experience the power of his healing spirit and his friendship. Jesus had a compassion that reached through death to his broken people. That same resurrection power can help us rise in the areas where suffering has held us down.

The man at the gate didn't rise alone. He was taken by the right hand and was raised up [26]. We can take comfort from the words from Isaiah 41, which says, 'the Lord your God takes hold of your right hand and says to you, Do not fear; I will help you' [27].

With God, we are always going to rise into new territory. The man at the gate, who was happy with a few coins, was given life to the fullest. That life included the opportunity to earn his own gold, but most importantly, he was raised into a new friendship with Jesus. Our intention may not be to 'rise,' but God makes that possible if we reach out towards all that he has available to us.

Walk

Post-c-section, the pain didn't disappear after I started to walk. In fact, each step was even more painful than the first. The truth is that I walked with the pain. But, over time, the open wound healed and became nothing more than a scar. Like the man at the gate who had to learn to walk again, we will also learn to walk again. Walking through life with loss is daunting. It changes the way we walk forever. It even changes the places we choose to tread. My testimony isn't that I was raised out of sorrow and never felt the pain again, but that I repeatedly keep rising despite this pain. I am continually choosing to walk with Jesus. God wants to take hold of your hand and help you rise again; he wants you to lean on him as a friend. If you have to make the choice to rise every hour, every day, or every week, there's room for that. The key is not to walk alone. In the same passage in Acts, the NLT says that the man, after being healed, began 'walking and leaping and praising God' [28]. The man had to know what it was to walk before he could leap. And so, remember to take one step at a time. Soon enough, you will get to the leaping and the praising.

References:

[22] Isaiah 40:31 (ESV): 'But those who keep waiting for the Lord will renew their strength. Then they'll soar on wings like eagles; they'll run and not grow weary; they'll walk and not grow tired.'

[23] Acts 3:1-6 (ESV): 'Peter directed his gaze at him, as did John, and said, "Look at us." And he fixed his attention on them, expecting to receive something from them. But Peter said, "I have no silver and gold, but what I do have I give to you. In the name of Jesus Christ of Nazareth, rise up and walk!"'

[24] Isaiah 40:11 (ESV): 'He will tend his flock like a shepherd; he will gather the lambs in his arms; he will carry them in his bosom, and gently lead those that are with young.'

[25] John 10:10 (ESV): 'I have come that they may have life, and have it to the full.'

[26] Acts 3:7-8 (NLT): 'Then Peter took the lame man by the right hand and helped him up. And as he did, the man's feet and ankles were instantly healed and strengthened. He jumped up, stood on his feet, and began to walk! Then, walking, leaping, and praising God, he went into the Temple with them.'

[27] Isaiah 41:13 (NIV): 'For I am the Lord your God who takes hold of your right hand and says to you, Do not fear; I will help you.'

CHAPTER 14

Returning Home

Home can symbolise many things for us. When Reuben died, a part of what I called home was washed away. It felt as though I had moved house and moved town. Everyone seemed different; I seemed different. Things that used to feel comfortable, like friendships and finding joy in the things I loved to do, no longer felt acceptable.

When I was five, my mum, my brother, and I became homeless. Though I was small, I remember it clearly. My dad had left us for another family. So, not only did we lose our home, but we lost him at the same time. My mum frantically tried to find us a place to call home to give us a sense of being protected, and whilst we needed that, I think I already knew that being together was more important than our surroundings.

As an adult, in my grief, I kept looking for a destination, a place of relief, joy, or contentment. But I found that what Jesus was calling me to wasn't a place, but himself. The promised land we are looking for is in Jesus! It says in Exodus 15:13: 'You have led in your steadfast love the people whom you have redeemed; you have guided them by your strength to your holy abode [home]' (ESV). In Psalm 90, we read: 'Lord, through all the generations you have been our home!'.

Where is Home?

The beautiful truth is that in all of our pain and loss, Jesus always guides us to Himself. He wants to be our home and our comfort. We may give the name 'home' to a physical building, a person we love, or a church family, but we won't find our true home in those things. Physical things can be crushed or knocked down, but if our home is Jesus, we will always have a strong foundation. No matter what comes our way, if we are built upon Jesus, nothing can tear us down.

Jesus tells us: 'Remain in me, as I also remain in you. No branch can bear fruit by itself; it must remain in the vine. Neither can you bear fruit unless you remain in me' [29]. The path you walk in grief is a path on which you can get to know Jesus intimately.

Jesus is so close to the broken-hearted. I have experienced this first-hand, even as a child. I remember walking down an isolated path when I was five years old. At the time I realised that my dad had gone for good. All that was left was the loneliness of my heart and a longing to be loved and accepted. I remember feeling abandoned, and then I heard a voice in my head. It was as faint as a whisper. It said that I was loved and special. I didn't know there was a God, and I hadn't been told that there was a God who loved me. All I knew was that I could trust the whispers I heard. Now I know them to be God's words over my life.

"You have to lead me in your love."

We are told: 'Love is patient, love is kind. It does not envy, it does not boast, it is not proud' [30]. God leads us with patience, kindness, and gentleness. Not with judgement, shame, or a sense of hurry. This means that when He guides us, He doesn't pick at everything you have said wrong or at the times you have held your heartache in and consequently caused others to suffer. Some of us, including myself, think that he's at our side forcing us towards the truth. In my experience, it is instead always a gentle nudge in the right direction.

Once, at our church in Watford, I felt like I was the only one grieving. I started to feel an overwhelming sense of sadness that made me feel isolated. It was as though I was the only one suffering. Jesus told me to lift my head and look around. He showed me that each of us share in some kind of suffering, whether it is our own or someone else's. I realised that our suffering shouldn't divide us, but unite us. The pain we feel connects us to each other and connects us to the Father God.

God has been guiding me in his love for my whole life—even before I could have put this into words. After my encounter with God as a five-year-old, God put a praying woman beside me, a friend of my mum's called Susan. She was the first person to tell me about Jesus, and she bought me a cross for one of my birthdays. When I look back, I can see God's hand in bringing her into my life. I became a Christian when I was seventeen. I was a troubled youth who had experienced abuse and inflicted self-harm. Did I know I needed God? No. My memory wouldn't even let me remember the voice that guided me when I was young. I needed a little more guidance. During this time in my life, an amazing friend called Joanne invited me to go to a beach party with her. I had a few drinks and, surprisingly, agreed to go to church with her the next day and decided I wanted to know Jesus.

God works in mysterious ways and leads with a fierce love. If you find yourself lost in grief and need to be led home, then I encourage you to pray this prayer; I encourage you to pray it even if you have never believed but feel encouraged and inspired by the love of Jesus:

Lord Jesus, please lead me in your steadfast love into my true home. Forgive me for my wanderings and my sins, and help me to live alongside you. Holy Spirit, you are welcome here, and I ask that I encounter the love of God. I pray I will find a friend in Jesus and know his comfort in my sorrows. Thank you for salvation, and for the love of Jesus. Amen!

References:

[29] John 15:4 (NIV): 'Remain in me, as I also remain in you. No branch can bear fruit by itself; it must remain in the vine. Neither can you bear fruit unless you remain in me.'

[30] 1 Corinthians 13:4-7 (NIV): 'Love is patient, love is kind. It does not envy, it does not boast, it is not proud.'

CHAPTER 15

Knowing Rejection

Suffering any kind of rejection is damaging in its own right, let alone suffering rejection while you're going through grief. During my darkest time, I went from being surrounded by my community to being rejected by them. People are human and broken, and not everyone can deal with the grief of others. Some—dare I say—are just too busy to mourn with those who are mourning. I experienced people trying to force me into healing in ways that didn't work. For example, some people were telling me I needed to smile more, which caused me more pain. I didn't feel the need to rush my healing. I had a long journey ahead, and it often felt like this was an inconvenience for some. It was around the six-month anniversary of losing Reuben when my closest friends at the time went silent on us as a family. I felt I had been labelled as damaged goods. I was confused as to why I was not being shown grace for my healing. I knew I was carrying my depression into all my conversations, and that can't have been easy for people, but I really needed people to stand by me.

A story Jesus once told really describes how I felt, and maybe this may speak into your similar situation. He speaks of a man who was going down from Jericho. He encountered some robbers who stripped him and beat him, and left him for dead. He lay there waiting for some kind of help, and his hopes started to rise when he saw a priest. Surely, he would be saved now! Unfortunately, rather than helping, the priest just passed by. Then a Levite began to approach him. Maybe things were looking up! The Levites were some of the most esteemed members of Israel, so they should know what it is to worship God. Sadly, that man walked past too. But, thankfully, the story gets better. A Samaritan saw the man and had compassion for him. He went to him, bound his wounds, poured oil and wine on them, took him to safety, and ensured that he had shelter and food. To truly understand the story, we need to remember that the Samaritans were the least likely to have helped because Samaritans were not really respected or liked. Maybe you know what it's like to be let down by the people you thought you could trust and then find that it's a stranger who offers you a helping hand or a kind word at the right moment.

The story of the good Samaritan is such a wonderful picture of the love of God shining through a human being. When we stand by someone who is hurting, we're committing to walking with them even when it's costly or inconvenient. The Samaritan gave up the comfort of his donkey and walked so the injured man could be carried, and he shared his food and water when his own supplies were likely to have been limited. All of this was just so he could keep someone he'd never met before alive.

Though you have known rejection, Jesus is the one who wants to put you on his donkey. Though you have been let down, Jesus will be the one who stands by you.

When my husband and I arrived home without our child, we needed space to heal. But, at the same time, a family member needed our help. They were desperate to live, but didn't have the strength to do so alone. Sometimes, the inconvenience doesn't make sense. Some would say we deserved to be selfish at that moment. I followed my instincts and believe to this day that a life was saved. In Romans 12:15, Paul instructs us to weep with those who are weeping. Love has the power to save lives. I am not sharing this to boast and say that I have never put myself first, because there are times that I have. There's grace for both paths. What I am saying is that there's always room for us to pick someone else up in their distress, even within our own suffering. Somehow, God gives us strength in our weakness—something we are reminded of in Psalm 73:26.

Leaning into a Loving God

The story of the good Samaritan teaches us so much about what it is to lean into a loving God with all we are. Rejection can make us focus on our own needs, and we can soon forget to make love our aim. The Samaritan first gave his thoughts to God, and therefore chose to see. Listening to God's heart is often seeing the need and then acting on the need. We are told in 1 Corinthians 12:27 to be the hands and feet of Jesus. In Matthew 25:34-45, Jesus says if we see someone in need, we should help as if it was Jesus himself. Seeing a need is where this behavior starts, but we must choose to look.

Secondly, it reminds us to give God everything we have—including our possessions, money, time, and energy. The Samaritan walked so the man could rest. He used his own money to see that the man would get fully better. When we give generously to other people's needs, it creates room for joy, and joy is healing. Giving where we lack can be quite daunting. For me, it was hard to give myself away. I felt so fatigued, and having to get up and be a mum, wife, and a colleague was a lot at times. At the same time, I wanted to change career—I really wanted to be a carer and work with elderly patients. I did so against the advice of my friends and family, and though it came at a cost, God gave me the strength to do it. I got to know some incredible people and was able to pray with a dear friend before she went home to be with Jesus. But one day it all got too much. Overnight, a sweet lady I was caring for was put on a breathing machine, and my mind went straight back to the NICU and to Reuben fighting for his life. I panicked and broke down. I was meant to be the one to rely on at this moment, but I couldn't handle the reality. The people I met were a gift to me, and I will never forget them. Despite breaking down, the career change was worth it. I encourage you not to be afraid of giving yourself, because when you are leaning into God's love, and when your aim is to love, you will never be left without strength.

The third thing I see in the Good Samaritan story is the sacrifice of identity or reputation. The Samaritan laid down what others thought of him and helped even though it wasn't expected of him. He showed kindness anyway. Giving God everything means laying down cultural expectations even though our identity has been wrapped in grief for so long. Leaning into God is leaving behind rejection and choosing to love others despite the differences we may have.

Learning to Forgive

There are three things I want to remind you about before I conclude this chapter. Firstly, forgiveness is a choice, not a feeling. Secondly, forgiveness doesn't condone the pain caused. Thirdly, forgiveness doesn't require you to remain in toxic or abusive relationships.

I imagine that the man who was beaten and left for dead had to forgive a lot of people—those who hurt him, and those who walked past without helping. It's a devastating story for this guy. It's one of those life-events that would keep you up at night raging. I'm sure we can all relate in some way—big or small! Forgiving isn't easy, and it took me a very long time to forgive the people who caused me pain. I would pray and pray for strength to forgive them.

The pain of rejection would get the better of me until I began to realise that I had the power of choice. Up to that point, my actions were led by the feeling of wanting to forgive, but one day I realised that I could choose to forgive despite how I feel. As a result, I could choose to not burden myself with other people's mistakes. For those who did not apologize, I wrote a letter to them that I never intended to send. It did me the world of good to say what I wanted to say and helped me move on and focus on what was important; on rebuilding some friendships and also letting some go. I am not under the illusion that forgiveness is a walk in the park, and I am the first to admit that the rage that is caused by rejection is hard to overcome. However, God is so gentle with us and wants to heal the heartbreak. He understands that forgiveness doesn't make what hurt you in the first place okay. God grieves with us, and he allows space for us to come to terms with our heartbreak. But He also offers us the gift of forgiveness, which allows us to know freedom.

SECTION FIVE

LEADING

CHAPTER 16

Joy and Grief

Joy is something that we can put on a pedestal—we can even make it an end goal for the journey of life. Sometimes, we allow it to mask the suffering we are going through, so that others cannot see it. Especially these days when joy seems to be identified with the perfect day or the perfect life, which we then share on media platforms. If you're not careful, you can end up painting a picture or a story that isn't entirely true. Ecclesiastes 3:4 tells us that "there is a time to weep and a time to laugh, a time to mourn and a time to dance" . In this chapter, I want to look at what it looks like to lead with joy whilst knowing grief.

I once longed to know joy like I did in the days before I knew loss. I waited for it, and I would count the moments till I would experience the rush of being satisfied. Still, I began to realise that there was joy in the deepest parts of my grief and that my contentment wasn't going to be found in a single rush of overwhelming relief. During WW2, Anne Frank famously wrote: "As long as people feel that kind of happiness within themselves, the joy of nature, health and much more besides, they'll always be able to recapture that happiness. Riches, prestige, everything can be lost. But the happiness in your own heart can only be dimmed; it will always be there, as long as you live, to make you happy again. Whenever you're feeling lonely or sad, try going to the loft on a beautiful day and looking outside. Not at the houses and the rooftops but at the sky. As long as you can look fearlessly at the sky, you'll know that you're pure within and will find happiness once more" .

Finding joy isn't a matter of deleting grief and replacing the suffering with the newest Instagram filter available. I believe that finding joy is about learning to look up from a place of grief for a few seconds to capture something more than grief. Anne Frank's analogy of looking up to the sky in the midst of injustice and war reminded me of when I would look up to God in moments of overwhelming sorrow. In those moments, I found joy in the knowledge that I wasn't alone; that there was a bigger picture than the picture I had based on my own understanding. When Jesus is a part of you, joy will also be. Joy is found in strength, and when we put our faith in God during a time of desperation, we find deeper joy. There's a beautiful proverb that complements the beauty of Anne Frank's quote. It reads: "Even in laughter the heart may ache, and the end of joy may be grief" (Proverbs 14:13, ESV) . Both joy and grief can often be found together. Understanding joy and grief is not so black and white as to involve simple definitions like "good emotions" or "bad emotions." It's more complex than that. Understanding joy and grief is about knowing the freedom to live with both while knowing that you will remain steadfast in Jesus.

Leading in Joy

In John 16:24 (LSB), we are told: "Ask and you will receive, so that your joy may be made complete" . Jesus explained to his disciples that he had to leave for the Holy Spirit to come (v5-8), but the disciples grieved. Jesus could see their grief and said their sadness would eventually turn into joy. He used the analogy of a woman giving birth. When her baby arrives, her suffering fades because of the joy of new life. Jesus was letting them know that even though they were grieving, there was a new joy coming that they could access through the Holy Spirit. The word "joy" in this passage means delight. The same word translated as "joy" in this passage is used in numerous passages in the Bible. A look at these will help us better understand the meaning of the word. For example, in Philippians 2:2, we read: "Then make my joy complete by being like-minded, having the same love, being one in spirit and of one mind" (NIV). Jesus, in John 17:13, prays: "Now I come to you; and these things I speak in the world so that they may have my joy" (LSB). Here, Jesus prays to the Father on behalf of the people that may have eternal life; he prays that they may know God the Father in Christ, and that they would be one as the Father is one with Christ. Having complete joy only happens when we are unified in the Father through Christ, and when we are unified together as a Church. I believe that leading with joy is about choosing to be one with God and living in his word in order to love one another. In other words, we have joy when we love one another in the way Jesus loved his people, which he did by humbling himself and dying for a people who didn't deserve it. So, by his love and grace, we receive joy.

In Matthew 25, Jesus tells a parable about what the kingdom of heaven looks like. A part of the parable talks about entering into the joy of the lord. The parable begins with a man who is about to travel to a far-away country. Beforehand, he entrusts his savings with three servants. He gives one servant five talents, another two talents, and another one talent, according to their ability. When the man returned from his travels, he was pleased to see that two servants had increased the value of what he had given them. He said to each, "Well done, good and faithful servants...Enter into the joy of your master" (ESV). Sadly, one of the servants had not chosen to invest in his money and instead buried it because he was afraid. As a result, he did not enter into the Lord's joy. This text spoke a lot about the meaning of joy for me. Firstly, I always thought joy was something I made for myself, not something I "entered." When we choose to invest with what little we have, we can expect joy. Investment might look like a prayer for someone who is also going through troubled times, or it looks like patience with a colleague at work while you journey through grief. Jesus has given us the Holy Spirit through Jesus Christ, so we have every fruit of the Spirit available to us. Investing looks like using this fruit, allowing it to grow, and allowing it to become stronger. Have we not seen through scripture that joy is fulfilled in Jesus, his word, and his presence? I believe that when we step out and share love, we create unity. Scripture says that joy is found when all these things are together. Joy will come through the lead of the Holy Spirit—even in our lack of understanding and loss. This fact should remind us that the Spirit of God is to lead in joy and not us in our own strength or ability.

If we return to John 16 and put ourselves in the disciples' shoes for a moment, we can understand their grief. They had to lose the physical person of Jesus. The loss of Jesus for them would mean knowing grief like we do when we lose someone we love. Lately, I have understood this grief more than I would have liked. I mentioned in a previous chapter that my mum had lung cancer; sadly, a while after, she passed away. My mum was someone I spoke to and saw daily. I miss the sound of her voice and her touch and smile. I think I would go as far as to say that the disciples felt the same loss. I can imagine the disciples eating together and doing their daily activities while missing Jesus.

The Message version, in John 16:21-23, reads: "When a woman gives birth, she has a hard time, there's no getting around it. But when the baby is born, there is joy in the birth" . The sadness you have right now is like that birthing pain, but the coming joy is commensurate. In the same passage, Jesus says, "When I see you again, you'll be full of joy, and it will be a joy no one can rob from you. You'll no longer be so full of questions. This is what I want you to do: Ask the Father for whatever is in keeping with the things I've revealed to you. Ask in my name, according to my will, and he'll most certainly give it to you. Your joy will be a river overflowing its banks!" Overflowing joy is one which impacts more than just yourself. It's when joy leaks out in your friendships and in your homes that it starts to make an impact. When your joy becomes more than just self-satisfaction and leads you to bring comfort and kindness to someone—that is what "leading with joy" looks like.

CHAPTER 17

To Build

After Reuben's death, I would wake up in the mornings with a tremendous feeling of dread, with the feeling that I didn't have the strength to be a mum, wife, and friend. I didn't even have the strength to brush my teeth and shower. I had lost the ability to do the simplest of tasks. I had to re-build my life piece by piece. Re-building my life again, on some days, looked like summoning up the strength to make porridge for my son, Elijah, or finding it in me to read him a book before bed. Re-building looked like choosing to forgive whenever someone didn't know how to love me well in my deep anguish. Re-building looked like allowing others to help in areas I couldn't cope with.

In the book of Genesis, we hear of a faithful man called Noah. God had requested that Noah build an ark because there would soon be a flood that would wipe out every living being. One of the key moments in the story is the fact that Noah would be saved through his choice in faith to build the ark. He saw no evidence of rain that would eventually cause the flood. However, he still chose to build the ark with the faith that it would safely carry him to dry land when the rains came.

When we choose to build new healthy rhythms into our lives—whether that be starting to forgive someone or making room to be honest about our pain—and when we choose to build these with God, we build our lives on the foundations of Jesus Christ.

The only thing left standing when the floods eventually came was the ark and everything in it. There is steadfastness available to us when everything seems lost. We have chosen to build a life on Jesus and not on our understanding of the storm. As the ark and those in it weathered the storm, they would have listened to and felt the force of the waves crashing against them. In grief, we also know what the waves sound like when they crash against us. We have felt the pressure and watched the sea of grief rising in front of us. We have experienced the fear of being in the middle of the storm, and, sometimes—if we are honest—have lost faith.

There is a lifeline and safety for us in the sea, just as the ark was for Noah, his family, and his animals as it brought them to a new and safe pasture. God creates a space for you to rest while he creates space for new life.

Build In Others

At the end of her life, I watched my mum build up other people's lives with kindness and gracious love. One day, she was rushed into urgent care after suffering cardiac arrest. She was told that she only had weeks to live and that the cancer had spread from her lungs to her heart. Whilst my mum was waiting for her family to arrive, she could hear a woman crying out in distress. My mum decided to shimmy over to this woman's side and tell her that Jesus was with her and that they didn't need to fear death. Then she prayed with her. Hearing about my mum's words to the woman in distress made me aware that re-building in a time of sorrow isn't just about me; it is about building as a church; it is about building together. It is when we build together that the kingdom of God is built, brick by brick, with the kindness and love given during our deepest turmoil.

When Noah built the boat, he did not build it for the approval of others. He built it because he trusted God was speaking to him. Similarly, my mum didn't rely on her own understanding or ability to stand. Why? God told Noah to build, and in the same spirit, God told my mum to trust in His love and not in people or in self-assurance. Noah chose to build in private even when building didn't look possible. God used what he built to fulfill hope; hope for a new start and a new life. Most importantly, what Noah gained out of building in faith was intimacy between himself and God. He learnt a valuable lesson: Do not build with one's own understanding, but with God's strength according to His will and way. Noah was on the path to something new, but it didn't come without a cost. When we want change, we cannot expect everything to stay the same as it was.

Leading

When we choose to build up other people's lives, even when it's costly— that, in my eyes, is leading. God can use your voice and actions to bring freedom to those around you. There is a story in scripture in which we are told that Moses left Egypt for a time after killing an Egyptian. After a while, God told him to return. We have read stories in other chapters about escaping Egypt; for Moses, Egypt was a place of pain. So why would he ever revisit such a place? For Moses, Egypt would have represented the slavery his people faced, the torment of his past, and it would be a reminder of all he lost, his shame, and his past mistakes. In Exodus 3, God called Moses from the burning bush, saying, "Moses, Moses!"' (v4, ESV). The text goes on: 'And he said, "Here I am." Then he said, "Do not come near; take your sandals off your feet, for the place on which you are standing is holy ground" (v4-5). I want you to remember this next part because it is profound. God explains to Moses that He has heard the cry of His people in Israel. God says, ''I know their sufferings, and I have come down to deliver them out of the hand of the Egyptians and to bring them up out of that land to a good and broad land, a land flowing in milk and honey" (v7-8). Then, in verse 10, God says to Moses '"Come, I will send you!"

God called Moses to holy ground in order to then send him out. He was sent with the sole purpose of answering the prayers and the weeping that flowed out from Egypt. You personally may no longer be grieving, but it doesn't mean you will never be sent to the grief of another on God's behalf so that you can be an answer to someone else's prayer. This time, when you go back, you will be strengthened to walk through the wilderness with those that need you to 'build' in their life.

I am astounded by the love of Jesus and his mercy, and I don't ever want to miss out on that, even if it's costly. 'Building' in someone else's life after yours has been torn down can be expensive when it comes to prayer, grace, love, kindness, humility, forgiveness, and time. Nevertheless, it's never a loss, nor wasted energy. I watched my mum battle cancer for eight years, but I also watched her build up life. I saw this while she looked after her dying dad for years, for example. Alongside that, she had a bed-bound friend for whom she would do shopping and cleaning every other day. I saw her give them time, energy, and money into building up the lives of others. At the end of her life, she didn't have a home or money to leave behind, but she left the greatest legacy: she showed us what it was to love without limits. The ark my mum built will carry on living in every heart and life affected by the love she willingly poured out.

There's a verse in Isaiah that perfectly communicates what I want to say. It reads: 'The Spirit of the Sovereign LORD is on me, because the LORD has anointed me to proclaim good news to the poor. He has sent me to bind up the broken-hearted, to proclaim freedom for the captives and release from darkness for the prisoners' (v1, NIV). We are called to GO out into the broken places of the world. Your experience of suffering can be wisdom for someone else; it could become the love of God flowing through you, and your story can provide the hope someone else needs. The pain you know will ignite prayers only you can pray, and it will light the flame of your unique compassion. You hold such a sacred gift, and I know suffering isn't necessarily a gift you would have wanted, but it is the source for what someone else needs.

Rain Will Come

When God instructed the rain to come down, the ark Noah had built remained above water. So will we. We will survive the long nights of mourning, the days of sadness, and the disappointment. Even when we have had no sleep and know there are another 15 hours to go until the next opportunity for rest, God will give us strength. Grace and mercy will be given to us when we have lost control and slammed a door (or two). God will pour out His peace when we are fearful. When we feel we are at breaking point, we can have confidence that the rain that is sometimes poured upon us will eventually stop!

One day, on my way home from the school pick-up, the kids and I got caught in torrential rain. Elijah, my son, asked, 'When it rains, does it mean that God is sad?' I reflected on the question until I replied, saying: 'The rain has a purpose for feeding the soil and bringing forth life...' I didn't even finish speaking before Elijah finished my sentence by saying, '...so we can breathe, because without trees there is no oxygen.'

The rains that fall upon us bring us challenges and sadness. The truth is that the rain sometimes confines and restricts us from stepping out of the boat we have built. But when the rain stops, we find that there is new life. We mustn't forget that the boat we build isn't our security; our security is in the one that gave us the strength to build. We cannot hold on to the seed that God has given us and expect it to grow. For that to happen, we have to lay down the seed in the soil.

Some of us are waiting for signs of life before stepping out. Noah had to wait for signs of life by sending a dove out. If it flew back, it meant it was not yet time to get off the boat and start rebuilding life on land. However, if it didn't return, that signified it was time to disembark and begin rebuilding on land. The difference between our story and the story of Noah is that Jesus went to the cross to give us ultimate life. As Jesus said, "It is finished" (John 19:30, NIV). He has won the victory. Jesus had gone before us and won the war that raged against us. Jesus is your sign of life, and there is life outside our minds' comfort. The ark's purpose was to get Noah to a certain point to start a new life. Once the ark had served its purpose, it was time to get out of the boat. God said to Noah, '"Come out of the ark"' (Genesis 8:16, ESV). It's your time to get out of the boat and shine the light that is within you. The gifts that God has given you carry you to a certain point, but there is a time to build a new life.

Acknowledgements

Writing a book has been a challenging and time-consuming process, especially as it has been a very vulnerable journey sharing my journey of personal loss. I could not have done it without the people who gave me strength and encouragement and told me I could when I felt I couldn't finish it.

A heartfelt thank you to my husband, Judah, who gave me space to process and patience to write this book. I am so grateful that Judah believed in me and encouraged me to keep going till I finished.

To my precious mum, she was the first person to read this book, and in her last days, she poured love, encouragement, and prayers into future readers. I am so thankful for her strength and prayers along the journey.

A massive thank you to Liza H, who edited my book and taught me so much about writing along the way. Her kindness and challenges gave me courage and inspired me even more to write.

To Ben Hammond, who is a dear friend, for giving so generously of his time to proofread my writing, and he never failed to encourage me along the way.

I want to give a heartfelt thank you to Claire, Shaun Lambert, and Alison Fenning who have been my biggest encouragers and I am grateful for all their wisdom, love, and care that they have shown.

To my dearest friends - Hannah, Faith, Susi, Sara, Amie, Rebecka, Tirzah, and Beth - who stood by me in times of struggle, who listened generously, and never failed to encourage me with kind words.

To my friends on the collective, who taught me bravery, always speaking life and wisdom into my life. I couldn't have done it without you.

To the wonderful Bev and Pete, who gave us a home in time of need and taught us to live with audacious faith.

To my dear friends Carole and Barry, who were there to hold our hands and pray for my family in our time of need.

To Pastor David Middleton, who inspired me to write and allowed me to find the gift of writing in my life.

To Joanne Barker, who invited me to church for the first time, introduced me to a precious community, and, most importantly, introduced me to the most important person in my life, Jesus.